A CHOICE OF
BURNS'S POEMS AND SONGS

14 February '94

As my Love
on Valentines Day.

yours aye.

I.

A Choice of
BURNS'S POEMS
AND SONGS

Introduced by
Sydney Goodsir Smith

faber and faber
LONDON · BOSTON

First published in this edition in 1966
by Faber and Faber Limited
3 Queen Square London WC1N 3AU

Printed in England by Clays Ltd, St Ives plc
All rights reserved

ISBN 0 571 06835 9

Contents

From *The Merry Muses of Caledonia*

Introduction

I

Robert Burns was born in the village of Alloway, near Ayr, on January 25th, 1759, and died in Dumfries on July 21st, 1796. His father was a poor tenant farmer of the old-fashioned rigid Calvinistic school, stern and moralising, independent of spirit and the soul of integrity. He gave his two sons as good an education as he could by hiring, in company with his neighbours, the services of a young schoolmaster, John Murdoch, who held his classes in turn in the cottages of the various subscribers. A recent writer has suggested that this poor peasant's son was better read for his age than the young Lord Byron thirty years later at Aberdeen Grammar School and Harrow. But poets generally educate themselves and on Burns's own testimony it was his old nurse, Betty Davidson, a kinswoman of his mother's, who "cultivated the latent seeds of Poesy" with her "tales and songs concerning devils, ghosts, fairies, brownies, witches, warlocks, spunkies, kelpies, elf candles, dead lights, wraiths, apparitions, cantraips, giants, inchanted towers, dragons and other trumpery". He needn't have been so condescending, for many years later all this trumpery bore marvellous fruit in "Tam o' Shanter".

The farming was never a success. The family moved from Alloway to nearby Lochlie and thence, on the death of their father in 1784, burdened with debt, to the neighbouring farm of Mossgiel. Here, freed from the restraint of his father's authority, young Rab Mossgiel (as the Scottish custom called him) spread his wings both socially and poetically.

Most of his greatest work, the satires, were written in the two years between 1784 and 1786. He wrote his first poem (a love song, of course) at the age of 14 while harvesting with young Nellie Kilpatrick from whose hand he had plucked a thorn. Thereafter he wrote about one a year till he was 20, in 1779, when the graph goes leaping up. It is of curious interest to watch a genius taking off for

7

the upper reaches: this is how it went. In 1780 he wrote half a dozen poems including the wonderful song, "Mary Morison", and in the next two years about a dozen. In 1783 he wrote eight, but next year the score jumps to eighteen, which includes the first of his satires, "The Twa Herds". 1785 is the great satirical year with twenty-six poems and 1786 the grand climacteric, his *annus mirabilis,* which produced fifty-nine, over one a week. He was now 27.

Alongside this outpouring of verse his private life had become increasingly complicated and hopeless. His illegitimate daughter, "dear bought Bess", had been born in 1785; he had been arraigned before the Kirk Session and made to thole his penance on the cutty stool along with his partner in crime, poor Lizzie Paton; he had "married" and been forced by her father to "repudiate" Jean Armour even though she was with child (so obnoxious to Armour were Burns's ways of life and thought); and he had "married" and bade a fond poetic farewell to ill-fated Mary Campbell ("Highland Mary") whom he had asked to accompany him to Jamaica; and, as usual with Burns, the new farm was another bad bargain.

It was under these manifold stresses and frustrations that he decided to cut his losses and seek his fortune in the West Indies. How serious this intention was, has been debated, but he certainly made enquiries about sailing, booked his passage and had a job waiting for him as book-keeper on an Ayrshire planter's estate at Port Antonio. Ostensibly to pay for this venture he decided to publish his poems many of which — the satires especially — had been circulating in manuscript among his friends. He got subscriptions at three shillings a head from about 350 people and had John Wilson, printer in Kilmarnock, run off 600 copies. The book, *Poems, Chiefly in the Scottish Dialect,* came out in July 1786 with immediate success and sold out in no time, giving the poet, after paying the printer, a net profit of £20. Jamaica was forgotten.

His book was acclaimed by the fashionable *literati* in Edinburgh (Henry Mackenzie, the "Man of Feeling", praised him in his weekly, *The Lounger*) and the poet was invited to the capital to prepare a new and enlarged edition. Here he largely wasted his time being wined and dined, but he made £200 from the new edition and sold the copyright to his printer Creech for another £100. Also, from Edinburgh he made tours in the Highlands and

8

the Borders jotting down fragments of old songs wherever he went — his new "craze", which was shortly to bear immortal fruit indeed. Back in the capital he conducted his tragi-comical pastoral affaire with Mrs Agnes Maclehose ("Clarinda"), a mildly sportive grass widow of sensibility and poetical pretensions, an affaire which, for all its folly, produced one of his greatest songs, "Ae Fond Kiss".

In 1788 with the money from his new edition he bought a new farm at Ellisland, near Dumfries, and at last settled down with and married the faithful Jean Armour who had presented him with a second pair of twins in the meanwhile. All this time he had also been trying to get a job in the Excise that would give him financial security.

Although his stay in Edinburgh was largely barren poetically, it had one important outcome. He met James Johnson, an engraver, "who has taken it into his head to publish a collection of all our songs set to music." Burns was to help him in "collecting the old poetry, or sometimes to a fine air to make a stanza, when it has no words". This was to occupy him, apart from occasional pieces, for the remaining ten years of his life. The results, some hundreds of songs that have gone round the world, were published in the six volumes of Johnson's *Scots Musical Museum* (1787–1803). Later, he contributed also to George Thomson's *Select Collection of Original Scotish Airs* (5 vols., 1793–1826). Today, for most people, Burns's fame is based on his songs in these two collections.

Alas, the new farm was no better than the others — "a poet's choice, not a farmer's" — but he had now landed a job as exciseman and in November of 1791 he sold up and moved into Dumfries. In the spring of this year, within a week of each other, Jean Armour had borne him a son, Nicol, and Ann Park of the Globe Tavern, Dumfries, a daughter, Elizabeth. Jean Armour, that great-hearted woman, merely remarked that "Our Rab should hae had twa wives" and nursed the two babes together. In Dumfries he became a prominent citizen; started a public lending library; wrote Prologues for the Theatre Royal (one of them hints that he was thinking of writing for the stage at this time); did his rounds as exciseman ("searching auld wives' barrels"); continued his convivial and amorous ways; was taken up by the local big wigs, the Riddells of Woodley Park, where he alternately courted Mrs Maria Riddell and was flung out for obstreperous behaviour; and got into trouble with the authorities for his outspoken sympathies with the French Republicans. ("May our success in the present war be equal to the justice of our cause!" was one of his toasts at a dinner.)

His health, never robust, was beginning to fail — rheumatic heart is the generally accepted diagnosis. In July 1796 his doctor advised sea bathing in the Solway. This probably finished him off and he returned to Dumfries a dying man. Even on his death bed his lyric genius did not desert him and his last poem, like his first one, was a love song, the poignant "O, wert thou in the cauld blast", written for young Jessie Lewars who was nursing him. The poet died on July 21st. While the funeral was taking place on the 25th, the heroic Jean was giving birth to his son Maxwell — a rather touching and most Burnsian coincidence. "The Lord giveth and the Lord taketh away."

II

In a weekly paper recently a writer recalled a fellow-matelot saying to him: "Poetry? Strictly an occupation for the upper and middle classes." It is one of Burns's distinctions in the history of literature that he transcends these limits. A century and a half after his death his songs are still sung and his poems quoted — and not only in Scotland — by the educated and the uneducated alike. He is still "pop", in fact, and internationally "pop". At the Tokio Olympic Games last year the grand finale ended with "Auld Lang Syne" which the Japanese believe is a Japanese song. The Chinese have it too. At the Burns Bicentenary in 1959, although our own G.P.O. refused, the Russians issued stamps to commemorate the occasion. Samuel Marshak's translation of Burns's poems is a constant best-seller in Russia, along with Shakespeare and Dickens. A host of phrases from his poems and songs have become proverbial: "A man's a man, for a' that", "Facts are chiels that winna ding", "To see oursels as ithers see us" — and so forth. You will not hear much Shakespeare or Milton quoted in an English pub or much Walt Whitman in an American, but in a pub in Scotland he is still part of the furniture, or rather I should say part of the family, for his fame has a markedly affectionate tinge about it in his own country.

This is probably due to the open humanity of the man. He puts so much of himself into his writings with all the inconsistencies common to us all and without glossing over the warts and back-slitherings. His character is there for all to see ("as open as a lighted inn") and he is endearing in his self revelation — humorous, gregarious, passionate, independent, sentimental, attitudinising, boastful, melancholic, indiscreet, patriotic, with a deep love of his brother man (always including sister woman) especially the unfortunate and the outcasts of society, equally at home on Helicon or sitting in the gutter.

His fame is certainly founded on the popularity of his songs, many of which (including "Auld Lang Syne") can hardly be called his own, being patched up versions of older ditties which had sometimes only the chorus surviving or a single first line or tune. He had an unerring ear for marrying words and music and to read the songs merely on the printed page is to lose half of the whole. The parts are truly inseparable.

His strongest voice, however, is found in the satires which transcend their immediate victims, objects or abuses by a universality of approach and a vitality of expression which render the opinions of a Holy Willie as up to date now as they were nearly two centuries ago. Even though the creed may die or change the Holy Willies in social and political life are still with us. The fact that these poems were written in a language or dialect spoken by comparatively few mortals on the face of the earth is another peculiarity of his fame.

It will be noticed that his best work is in Scots. Though he wrote a lot in English he was never at ease with that language and generally quite unsuccessful in verse though his letters show that he could write excellent if somewhat stilted and mannered prose — but this was the style of the age. "These English songs gravel me to death — I have not that command of the language that I have of my native tongue", he wrote to Thomson, sending him some verses. "In fact, I think my ideas are more barren in English than in Scottish. — I have been at 'Duncan Gray' to dress it in English, but all I can do is deplorably stupid."

By continuing the work of Allan Ramsay and Robert Fergusson (whose use of Scots was against the anglicising current of the eighteenth century in Scotland) he placed Scots once again among the literary languages of Europe as it had been in the fifteenth and sixteenth centuries with Dunbar, Henryson, Douglas and Lyndsay, and even in the seventeenth with the Ballads, a position it had largely abdicated following the anglicisation and provincialisation of Scottish life and thought after the Union of the Crowns in 1603 and the removal of the cultural centre, the court, to London. This process was much speeded up after the Parliamentary Union of 1707 and the consequent ingestion of Scottish political life by Westminster. Ramsay and Fergusson had resisted the trend (they were both Jacobite in sympathy, by the way) and it was coming upon a copy of Fergusson's poems when he was twenty-three that set Burns on the road he was to follow. To those who complain that Scots is too difficult I would quote Ezra Pound regarding Chaucer: "Anyone who is too lazy to master the comparatively small glossary necessary to understand Chaucer deserves to be shut out from the reading of good books forever." *Verb. sap.*

Burns has received some heavy battering from twentieth-century critics. We have been told that he has no original message ("he deals only in the great platitudes"); that he was "but the singer of a parish"; that he originated nothing technically in his craft or art but merely brought to a final flowering the work of generations of forerunners; that he didn't even write in the language of his day but often used a vocabulary that had already become obsolete — a language, by the way, that his friends among the *literati* were always urging him to drop for the more generally understood English; that his famous songs were not original (very many of the most famous were, of course); that his thought was very confused ("Jacobite and Jacobin" is the usual phrase) — and so on.

Yet despite all this he gets through and gets through to don and docker equally, as to true-blue and red, and crosses seas and continents with ease. The best Burns scholarship is by a Frenchman (Angellier), two Americans (Snyder and DeLancey Ferguson), an Englishman (Henley), a German (Hecht), two Russians (Marshak and Mme Elistratova) and two Scots (Daiches and Crawford), and he has been translated into every civilised language in the world — including Chinese (I have a copy). He is one of a very few poets who have ever achieved such a universal audience.

III

There is no definitive edition of Burns's works; the Centenary Edition by W. E. Henley and T. F. Henderson (1896) is the best so far. The difficulty is that he was always copying out poems for his friends and the many MSS vary in both wording and spelling, as do even the printed texts he prepared himself. In the Edinburgh editions he anglicised his spelling a good deal (but not consistently), presumably to cater for what he thought of as a more sophisticated public. The Kilmarnock, for instance, often (but not always) keeps such old Scots forms as the *-an* or *-and* ending to the present participle (compare French *-ant*) and *-it* or *-et* for the past. The latter, when anglicised to *-ed*, should generally be sounded as a syllable — hence the frequent *-'d* when it is elided; I have sometimes taken the liberty of accenting it *-èd* for the reader's convenience, though the scansion will generally demand the syllable obviously enough.

Most of these selections come from one or other of the first two Edinburgh editions, the *Scots Musical Museum* and the Centenary Edition. Among the exceptions are two from the Kilmarnock edition ("The Twa Dogs" and "Scotch Drink"), "Holy Willie's Prayer" from the Glenriddell MSS, and the small clutch of bawdy songs at the end from *The Merry Muses of Caledonia* (W. H. Allen 1965), originally published anonymously, probably in Edinburgh, a year after the poet's death. For those loyal souls who doubt Burns's authorship of these bagatelles, as he called them, the evidence is all assembled in the notes and introductions to the Allen edition, to which I refer them.

SYDNEY GOODSIR SMITH

Edinburgh 1965

A Man's a Man For A' that

Is there, for honest poverty
  That hangs his head, and a' that;
The coward-slave, we pass him by,
  We dare be poor for a' that!
For a' that, and a' that,
  Our toils obscure, and a' that,
The rank is but the guinea's stamp,
  The man's the gowd for a' that.

What though on hamely fare we dine,
  Wear hoddin grey, and a' that;
Gie fools their silks, and knaves their wine,
  A man's a man for a' that:
For a' that, and a' that,
  Their tinsel show, and a' that;
The honest man, though e'er sae poor,
  Is king o' men for a' that.

Ye see yon birkie, ca'd a lord,
  Wha struts, and stares, and a' that;
Though hundreds worship at his word,
  He's but a coof for a' that:
For a' that, and a' that,
  His ribband, star, and a' that,
The man of independent mind,
  He looks and laughs at a' that.

A prince can mak a belted knight,
  A marquis, duke, and a' that;
But an honest man's aboon his might,
  Gude faith, he mauna fa' that!

gowd, gold; *hamely*, homely; *hoddin grey*, coarse grey woollen; *gie*, give;
birkie, fellow; *ca'd*, called; *coof*, fool; *aboon*, above; *mauna fa'*, better not try.

For a' that, and a' that,
   Their dignities, and a' that,
The pith o' sense, and pride o' worth,
   Are higher ranks than a' that

Then let us pray that come it may,
   As come it will for a' that,
That sense and worth, o'er a' the earth,
   May bear the gree, and a' that.
For a' that, and a' that,
   Its comin yet for a' that,
That man to man, the warld o'er,
   Shall brothers be for a' that.

1794

bear the gree, have the first place.

The Jolly Beggars * — *A Cantata*

RECITATIVO

When lyart leaves bestrow the yird,
Or wavering like the bauckie-bird,
   Bedim cauld Boreas' blast;
When hailstanes drive wi' bitter skyte,
And infant frosts begin to bite,
   In hoary cranreuch drest;
Ae night at e'en a merry core
   O' randie, gangrel bodies,

lyart, faded; *yird*, earth; *bauckie-bird*, the bat; *skyte*, dash; *cranreuch*, hoar frost; *core*, company; *gangrel*, vagrant.

* The original title of this "puissant and splendid production", to quote Matthew Arnold, was "Love and Liberty". Burns intended to print this in his Edinburgh edition but was dissuaded. It was first published as a tract a year after his death, 1799.

16

In Poosie-Nansie's held the splore,
To drink their orra duddies;
Wi' quaffing an' laughing,
They ranted an' they sang,
Wi' jumping an' thumping,
The vera girdle rang.

First, neist the fire, in auld red rags,
Ane sat, weel brac'd wi' mealy bags,
And knapsack a' in order;
His doxy lay within his arm;
Wi' usquebae an' blankets warm
She blinkit on her sodger;
An' aye he gies the tozie drab
The tither skelpin kiss,
While she held up her greedy gab,
Just like an aumous dish;
Ilk smack still did crack still,
Just like a cadger's whip;
Then staggering an' swaggering
He roar'd this ditty up —

AIR

Tune: "Soldier's Joy"

I am a son of Mars who have been in many wars,
And show my cuts and scars wherever I come;
This here was for a wench, and that other in a trench,
When welcoming the French at the sound of the drum.
Lal de daudle, etc.

Poosie, Pussie; *splore*, party, spree: *orra duddies*, lit. their worthless rags (i.e. drink the clothes off their backs: cf. "betting", put your shirt on it); *girdle*, griddle; *neist*, next; *mealy*, meal; *usquebae*, whisky; *sodger*, soldier; *tozie*, tipsy; *tither*, the other; *skelpin*, smacking; *aumous*, alms, i.e. begging bowl; *Ilk*, each, every; *cadger*, carrier.

17

My prenticeship I past where my leader breath'd his last,
  When the bloody die was cast on the heights of Abram:
And I servèd out my trade when the gallant game was play'd,
  And the Moro low was laid at the sound of the drum.

I lastly was with Curtis among the floating batt'ries,
  And there I left for witness an arm and a limb;
Yet let my country need me, with Elliot to head me,
  I'd clatter on my stumps at the sound of a drum.

And now tho' I must beg, with a wooden arm and leg,
  And many a tatter'd rag hanging over my bum,
I'm as happy with my wallet, my bottle and my callet,
  As when I used in scarlet to follow a drum.

What tho', with hoary locks, I must stand the winter shocks,
  Beneath the woods and rocks oftentimes for a home,
When the tother bag I sell, and the tother bottle tell,
  I could meet a troop of Hell, at the sound of a drum.

RECITATIVO

He ended; and the kebars sheuk,
  Aboon the chorus roar;
While frighted rattons backward leuk,
  An' seek the benmost bore:
A fairy fiddler frae the neuk,
  He skirl'd out, encore!
But up arose the martial chuck,
  An' laid the loud uproar.

AIR

Tune: "Sodger Laddie"

I once was a maid, tho' I cannot tell when,
  And still my delight is in proper young men:

callet, whore; *kebars sheuk*, rafters shook; *rattons*, rats; *benmost*, inmost;
bore, hole, chink; *fairy*, "away with the fairies"; *neuk*, corner; *skirl'd*,
yelled; *chuck*, chick.

18

Some one of a troop of dragoons was my daddie,
No wonder I'm fond of a sodger laddie.
                    Sing, lal de lal, etc.

The first of my loves was a swaggering blade,
To rattle the thundering drum was his trade;
His leg was so tight, and his cheek was so ruddy,
Transported I was with my sodger laddie.

But the godly old chaplain left him in the lurch;
The sword I forsook for the sake of the church:
He ventur'd the soul, and I riskèd the body,
'Twas then I proved false to my sodger laddie.

Full soon I grew sick of my sanctified sot,
The regiment at large for a husband I got;
From the gilded spontoon to the fife I was ready,
I askèd no more but a sodger laddie.

But the peace it reduc'd me to beg in despair,
Till I met my old boy in a Cunningham fair;
His rags regimental, they flutter'd so gaudy,
My heart it rejoic'd at a sodger laddie.

And now I have liv'd — I know not how long,
But still I can join in a cup and a song;
And whilst with both hands I can hold the glass steady,
Here's to thee, my hero, my sodger laddie.

RECITATIVO

Poor Merry-Andrew, in the neuk,
    Sat guzzling wi' a tinkler-hizzie;
They mind't na wha the chorus teuk,
    Between themsels they were sae busy:

sodger, soldier; *tight,* trim; *tinkler hizzie,* tinker hussy; *mind't na,* cared not;
teuk, took.

At length, wi' drink an' courting dizzy,
He stoiter'd up an' made a face;
　　Then turn'd an' laid a smack on Grizzie,
Syne tun'd his pipes wi' grave grimace.

Tune: "Auld Sir Symon"

Sir Wisdom's a fool when he's fou;
　　Sir Knave is a fool in a session;
He's there but a prentice I trow,
　　But I am a fool by profession.

My grannie she bought me a beuk,
　　An' I held awa to the school;
I fear I my talent misteuk,
　　But what will ye hae of a fool?

For drink I would venture my neck;
　　A hizzie's the half of my craft;
But what could ye other expect
　　Of ane that's avowedly daft?

I ance was tied up like a stirk,
　　For civilly swearing and quaffin;
I ance was abus'd i' the kirk,
　　For towsing a lass i' my daffin.

Poor Andrew that tumbles for sport,
　　Let naebody name wi' a jeer;
There's ev'n, I'm tauld, i' the Court
　　A tumbler ca'd the Premier.

Observ'd ye yon reverend lad
　　Mak faces to tickle the mob;
He rails at our mountebank squad, —
　　It's rivalship just i' the job.

stoiter'd, staggered; *smack,* kiss; *Syne,* then; *fou,* drunk; *beuk,* book;
ance, once; *stirk,* bullock; *towsing,* un-silken dalliance; *daffin,* petting;
tauld, told; *ca'd,* called.

And now my conclusion I'll tell,
    For faith I'm confoundedly dry;
The chiel that's a fool for himsel',
    Guid Lord! he's far dafter than I.

RECITATIVO

Then niest out spak a raucle carlin,
Wha kent fu' weel to cleek the sterlin;
For monie a pursie she had hooked,
An' had in mony a well been douked:
Her love had been a Highland laddie,
But weary fa' the waeful woodie!
Wi' sighs and sobs she thus began
To wail her braw John Highlandman.

AIR

Tune: "O an ye were dead, Guidman"

A Highland lad my love was born,
The Lalland laws he held in scorn;
But he still was faithfu' to his clan,
My gallant, braw John Highlandman.

Chorus
    Sing hey my braw John Highlandman!
    Sing ho my braw John Highlandman!
    There's not a lad in a' the lan'
    Was match for my John Highlandman.

With his philibeg an' tartan plaid,
An' guid claymore down by his side,
The ladies' hearts he did trepan,
My gallant, braw John Highlandman.
    Sing hey, etc.

chiel, chap; *niest*, next; *spak*, spoke; *raucle carlin*, coarse trollop; *Wha kent* . . . , an adept pickpocket; *douked*, ducked; *weary fa'* . . . , curses on the gallows tree; *Lalland*, Lowland; *philibeg*, kilt; *trepan*, seduce.

We rangèd a' from Tweed to Spey,
An' liv'd like lords an' ladies gay;
For a Lalland face he fearèd none, —
My gallant, braw John Highlandman.
      Sing hey, etc.

They banish'd him beyond the sea.
But ere the bud was on the tree,
Adown my cheeks the pearls ran,
Embracing my John Highlandman.
      Sing hey, etc.

But, och! they catch'd him at the last,
And bound him in a dungeon fast:
My curse upon them every one,
They've hang'd my braw John Highlandman!
      Sing hey, etc.

And now a widow, I must mourn
The pleasures that will ne'er return:
No comfort but a hearty can,
When I think on John Highlandman.
      Sing hey, etc.

RECITATIVO

A pigmy scraper wi' his fiddle,
Wha us'd to trystes an' fairs to driddle,
Her strapping limb and gausy middle
      (He reach'd nae higher)
Had hol'd his heartie like a riddle,
      An' blawn't on fire.

Wi' hand on hainch, and upward e'e,
He croon'd his gamut, one, two, three,

Lalland, Lowland; *trystes*, markets, occasions; *driddle*, toddle; *gausy*, buxom; *riddle*, sieve; *blawn't*, blown it; *hainch*, haunch; *e'e*, eye.

22

Then in an arioso key,
               The wee Apollo
Set off wi' allegretto glee
               His giga solo.

AIR

Tune: "Whistle owre the lave o't"

Let me ryke up to dight that tear,
An' go wi' me an' be my dear;
An' then your every care an' fear
    May whistle owre the lave o't.

Chorus
I am a fiddler to my trade,
    An' a' the tunes that e'er I played,
The sweetest still to wife or maid,
        Was whistle owre the lave o't.

At kirns an' weddins we'se be there,
An' O sae nicely's we will fare!
We'll bowse about till Daddie Care
    Sing whistle owre the lave o't.
        I am, etc.

Sae merrily's the banes we'll pyke,
An' sun oursel's about the dyke;
An' at our leisure, when ye like,
    We'll whistle owre the lave o't.
        I am, etc.

But bless me wi' your heav'n o' charms,
An' while I kittle hair on thairms,
Hunger, cauld, an' a' sic harms,
    May whistle owre the lave o't.
        I am, etc.

ryke, reach; *dight*, wipe; *owre*, over; *lave o't*, rest of it; *kirn*, harvest home; *we'se*, we'll; *bowse*, booze; *banes*, bones; *pyke*, pick bare; *dyke*, wall; *kittle*, tickle; *thairms*, catgut, fiddlestrings; *sic*, such.

23

Her charms had struck a sturdy caird,
    As weel as poor gut-scraper;
He taks the fiddler by the beard,
    An' draws a roosty rapier —
He swoor by a' was swearing worth,
    To speet him like a pliver,
Unless he would from that time forth
    Relinquish her for ever:

Wi' ghastly e'e, poor tweedle-dee
    Upon his hunkers bended,
An' pray'd for grace wi' ruefu' face,
    An' so the quarrel ended.
But tho' his little heart did grieve
    When round the tinkler prest her,
He feign'd to snirtle in his sleeve,
    When thus the caird address'd her:

AIR

Tune: "Clout the Cauldron"

My bonie lass, I work in brass,
    A tinkler is my station:
I've travell'd round all Christian ground
    In this my occupation;
I've taen the gold, an' been enrolled
    In many a noble squadron;
But vain they search'd when off I march'd
    To go an' clout the cauldron.

Despise that shrimp, that wither'd imp,
    With a' his noise an' cap'rin;
An take a share wi' those that bear
    The budget and the apron!

caird, tinker; *roosty*, rusty; *speet*, spit; *pliver*, plover; *e'e*, eye; *hunkers*, haunches; *tinkler*, tinker; *snirtle*, snigger; *taen*, taken; *clout*, patch; *budget*, satchel.

24

And by that stowp, my faith an' houp,
    And by that dear Kilbaigie,
If e'er ye want, or meet wi' scant,
    May I ne'er weet my craigie.

RECITATIVO

The caird prevail'd — th' unblushing fair
    In his embraces sunk;
Partly wi' love o'ercome sae sair,
    An' partly she was drunk:
Sir Violino, with an air
    That show'd a man o' spunk,
Wish'd unison between the pair,
    An' made the bottle clunk
                To their health that night.

But hurchin Cupid shot a shaft,
    That play'd a dame a shavie —
The fiddler rak'd her, fore and aft,
    Behint the chicken cavie.
Her lord, a wight of Homer's craft,
    Tho' limpin wi' the spavie,
He hirpl'd up, an' lap like daft,
    An' shor'd them *Dainty Davie*
                O' boot that night.

He was a care-defying blade
    As ever Bacchus listed!
Tho' Fortune sair upon him laid,
    His heart, she ever miss'd it.

houp, hope; *Kilbaigie*, a whisky; *weet*, wet; *craigie*, throat; *sae sair*, so strongly; *shavie*, trick; *Behint*, behind; *cavie*, coop; *spavie*, spavin; *hirpl'd*, limped; *lap*, leapt; *an' shor'd . . .*, and promised them a return match gratis; *sair*, sorely.

He had no wish but — to be glad,
  Nor want but — when he thirsted;
He hated nought but — to be sad,
  An' thus the muse suggested
              His sang that night.

AIR

Tune: "For a' that, an' a' that"

I am a Bard of no regard,
  Wi' gentle folks an' a' that;
But Homer-like, the glowrin byke,
  Frae town to town I draw that.

Chorus
      For a' that, an' a' that,
        An' twice as muckle's a' that;
      I've lost but ane, I've twa behin',
        I've wife eneugh for a' that.

I never drank the Muses' stank,
  Castalia's burn, an' a' that;
But there it streams an' richly reams,
  My Helicon I ca' that.
           For a' that, etc.

Great love I bear to a' the fair,
  Their humble slave an' a' that;
But lordly will, I hold it still
  A mortal sin to thraw that.
           For a' that, etc.

In raptures sweet, this hour we meet,
  Wi' mutual love an' a' that;
But for how lang the flie may stang,
  Let inclination law that.
           For a' that, etc.

glowrin byke, goggling mob; *stank*, pool, ditch; *reams*, foams; *thraw*, thwart; *stang*, sting; *law*, rule.

Their tricks an' craft hae put me daft,
    They've taen me in, an' a' that;
But clear your decks, and here's — "The Sex!"
    I like the jads for a' that.

Chorus
For a' that, an' a' that,
    An' twice as muckle's a' that;
My dearest bluid, to do them guid,
    They're welcome till't for a' that.

RECITATIVO

So sang the bard — and Nansie's wa's
Shook with a thunder of applause,
    Re-echo'd from each mouth!
They toom'd their pocks, they pawn'd their duds,
They scarcely left to co'er their fuds,
    To quench their lowin drouth:
Then owre again, the jovial thrang
    The poet did request
To lowse his pack an' wale a sang,
    A ballad o' the best;
        He rising, rejoicing,
            Between his twa Deborahs,
        Looks round him, an' found them
            Impatient for the chorus.

AIR

Tune: "Jolly Mortals, fill your Glasses"

See the smoking bowl before us,
    Mark our jovial ragged ring!
Round and round take up the chorus,
    And in raptures let us sing —

taen, taken; *jads*, jades; *till't*, to it; *wa's*, walls; *toom'd*, emptied; *pocks*,
pockets; *duds*, rags; *co'er*, cover; *fuds*, backsides; *lowin*, blazing; *drouth*,
thirst; *owre*, over; *thrang*, throng; *lowse*, put off; *wale*, choose; *sang*, song.

Chorus

A fig for those by law protected !
Liberty's a glorious feast !
Courts for cowards were erected,
Churches built to please the priest.

What is title, what is treasure,
What is reputation's care?
If we lead a life of pleasure,
'Tis no matter how or where !
A fig for, etc.

With the ready trick and fable,
Round we wander all the day;
And at night in barn or stable,
Hug our doxies on the hay.
A fig for, etc.

Does the train-attended carriage
Thro' the country lighter rove?
Does the sober bed of marriage
Witness brighter scenes of love?
A fig for, etc.

Life is all a variorum,
We regard not how it goes;
Let them cant about decorum,
Who have character to lose.
A fig for, etc.

Here's to budgets, bags and wallets !
Here's to all the wandering train.
Here's our ragged brats and callets,
One and all cry out, Amen !

budgets, satchels; *callets*, trollops.

A fig for those by law protected!
Liberty's a glorious feast!
Courts for cowards were erected,
Churches built to please the priest.

November 1785

Address to the Unco Guid

OR THE RIGIDLY RIGHTEOUS

My son, these maxims make a rule,
And lump them ay thegither;
The Rigid Righteous *is a fool,*
The Rigid Wise *anither:*
The cleanest corn that e'er was dight
May hae some pyles o' caff in;
So ne'er a fellow-creature slight
For random fits o' daffin.

SOLOMON: *Eccles.* ch. vii, ver. 16

I

O ye wha are sae guid yoursel,
 Sae pious and sae holy,
Ye've nought to do but mark and tell
 Your neebours' fauts and folly!
Whase life is like a weel-gaun mill,
 Supply'd wi' store o' water,
The heapet happer's ebbing still,
 An' still the clap plays clatter.

II

Hear me, ye venerable Core,
 As counsel for poor mortals,
That frequent pass douce Wisdom's door
 For glaikit Folly's portals;

dight, sifted; *caff,* chaff; *daffin,* larking; *neebours',* neighbours'; *fauts,*
faults; *weel-gaun,* well-going; *happer,* hopper; *clap,* clapper of a mill;
Core, company; *douce,* sober; *glaikit,* giddy.

29

I, for their thoughtless, careless sakes,
    Would here propone defences,
Their donsie tricks, their black mistakes,
    Their failings and mischances.

III

Ye see your state wi' theirs compar'd
    And shudder at the niffer,
But cast a moment's fair regard,
    What makes the mighty differ;
Discount what scant occasion gave,
    That purity ye pride in,
And (what's aft mair than a' the lave)
    Your better art o' hiding.

IV

Think, when your castigated pulse
    Gies now and then a wallop,
What ragings must his veins convulse,
    That still eternal gallop:
Wi' wind and tide fair i' your tail,
    Right on ye scud your sea-way;
But in the teeth o' baith to sail,
    It makes an unco leeway.

V

See Social-life and Glee sit down,
    All joyous and unthinking,
Till, quite transmugrify'd, they're grown
    Debauchery and Drinking:
O would they stay to calculate
    Th' eternal consequences;
Or your more dreaded hell to state,
    Damnation of expences!

propone, put forward; *donsie*, unlucky; *niffer*, exchange; *aft*, often; *lave*, rest; *baith*, both; *unco*, awful.

VI

Ye high, exalted, virtuous Dames,
  Ty'd up in godly laces,
Before ye gie poor Frailty names,
  Suppose a change o' cases;
A dear-lov'd lad, convenience snug,
  A treacherous inclination —
But, let me whisper i' your lug,
  Ye're aiblins nae temptation.

VII

Then gently scan your brother Man,
  Still gentler sister Woman;
Tho' they may gang a kennin wrang,
  To step aside is human:
One point must still be greatly dark,
  The moving *Why* they do it;
And just as lamely can ye mark,
  How far perhaps they rue it.

VIII

Who made the heart, 'tis *He* alone
  Decidedly can try us,
He knows each chord its various tone,
  Each spring its various bias:
Then at the balance let's be mute,
  We never can adjust it;
What's *done* we partly may compute,
  But know not what's *resisted*.

1786

gie, give; *lug*, ear; *aiblins*, maybe; *kennin*, a thought, a little.

The Twa Dogs

'T was in that place o' Scotland's isle,
That bears the name o' auld king Coil,
Upon a bonie day in June,
When wearing thro' the afternoon,
Twa Dogs, that were na thrang at hame,
Forgather'd ance upon a time.

 The first I'll name, they ca'd him Caesar,
Was keepet for His Honor's pleasure;
His hair, his size, his mouth, his lugs,
Shew'd he was nane o' Scotland's dogs,
But whalpet some place far abroad,
Where sailors gang to fish for Cod.

 His locked, letter'd, braw brass-collar
Shew'd him the gentleman an' scholar;
But tho' he was o' high degree,
The fient a pride na pride had he,
But wad hae spent an hour caressan,
Ev'n wi' a tinkler-gypsey's messan:
At Kirk or Market, Mill or Smiddie,
Nae tawted tyke, tho' e'er sae duddie,
But he wad stan't, as glad to see him,
An' stroan't on stanes an' hillocks wi' him.

 The tither was a ploughman's collie,
A rhyming, ranting, raving billie,
Wha for his friend an' comrade had him,
And in his freaks had Luath ca'd him,
After some dog in Highland sang,*
Was made lang syne, lord knows how lang.

Coil, Kyle, in Ayrshire; *thrang*, busy; *lugs*, ears; *fient,* devil; *tinkler,* tinker; *messan*, mongrel; *smiddie*, smithy; *tawted*, matted; *duddie*, ragged; *stan't*, have stood; *stroan't*, piddled; *freak*, fancy.

  * Cuchullin's dog in Ossian's *Fingal*. (Burns's note.)

He was a gash, and faithfu' tyke,
As ever lap a sheugh or dyke.
His honest, sonsie, baws'nt face,
Aye gat him friends in ilka place;
His breast was white, his towzie back
Weel clad wi' coat o' glossy black;
His gawsie tail, wi' upward curl,
Hung owre his hurdies wi' a swirl.

Nae doubt but they were fain o' ither,
An' unco pack an' thick thegither;
Wi' social nose whyles snuff'd an' snowket;
Whyles mice and modewurks they howket;
Whyles scour'd awa in lang excursion,
An' worry'd ither in diversion;
Till tir'd at last wi' mony a farce,
They set them down upon their arse,
An' there began a lang digression
About the lords o' the creation.

CAESAR

I've aften wonder'd, honest Luath,
What sort o' life poor dogs like you have;
An' when the gentry's life I saw,
What way poor bodies liv'd ava.

Our Laird gets in his racked rents,
His coals, his kane, an a' his stents:
He rises when he likes himsel;
His flunkies answer at the bell;
He ca's his coach; he ca's his horse;
He draws a bonie, silken purse

gash, wise; lap, leapt; sheugh, ditch; dyke, wall; sonsie, pleasant; baws'nt,
white-striped; gawsie, handsome; hurdies, hind-quarters; pack, close;
snowket, scented; Whyles, sometimes; modewurks, moles; howket, dug up;
ava, at all; kane, rents in kind; stents, dues; ca's, calls.

B.P.S

As lang's my tail, whare thro' the steeks,
The yellow letter'd Geordie keeks.

Frae morn to een it's nought but toiling,
At baking, roasting, frying, boiling;
An' tho' the gentry first are steghan,
Yet ev'n the ha' folk fill their peghan
Wi' sauce, ragouts, an' sic like trashrie,
That's little short o' downright wastrie.
Our Whipper-in, wee blastet wonner,
Poor worthless elf, it eats a dinner,
Better than ony Tenant-man
His Honor has in a' the lan':
An' what poor Cot-folk pit their painch in,
I own it's past my comprehension.

LUATH

Trowth, Caesar, whyles their fash't enough;
A Cotter howkan in a sheugh,
Wi' dirty stanes biggan a dyke,
Bairan a quarry an' sic like,
Himsel, a wife, he thus sustains,
A smytrie o' wee, duddie weans,
An' nought but his han'-daurk, to keep
Them right an' tight in thack an' raep.

An' when they meet wi' sair disasters,
Like loss o' health or want o' masters,
Ye maist wad think, a wee touch langer,
An' they maun starve o' cauld an' hunger:

steeks, stitches; *keeks*, peeps; *steghan*, stuffing; *ha' folk*, servants; *peghan*, stomach; *wonner*, wonder; *Cot-folk*, cottagers; *pit their painch in*, put in their stomach; *fash't*, worried; *howkan*, digging; *sheugh*, ditch; *biggan*, building; *Bairan*, clearing; *sic*, such; *smytrie*, swarm; *duddie*, ragged; *han'-daurk*, handwork; *thack*, thatch; *raep*, rope; *sair*, severe; *maist wad*, almost would; *maun*, must.

34

But how it comes, I never kent yet,
They're maistly wonderfu' contented;
An' buirdly chiels, and clever hizzies,
Are bred in sic a way as this is.

CAESAR

But then, to see how ye're negleket,
How huff'd, an' cuff'd, an' disrespeket!
Lord man, our gentry care as little
For delvers, ditchers, an' sic cattle;
They gang as saucy by poor folk,
As I wad by a stinkan brock.

I've notic'd on our Laird's court-day,
An' mony a time my heart's been wae,
Poor tenant bodies, scant o' cash,
How they maun thole a factor's snash;
He'll stamp and threaten, curse an' swear,
He'll apprehend them, poind their gear;
While they maun stan', wi' aspect humble,
An' hear it a', an' fear an' tremble!

I see how folk live that hae riches;
But surely poor folk maun be wretches!

LUATH

They're no sae wretched's ane wad think;
Tho' constantly on poortith's brink,
They're sae accustom'd wi' the sight,
The view o't gies them little fright.

buirdly, burly; *chiels*, fellows; *hizzies*, hussies; *huff'd*, bullied; *stinkan brock*, stinking badger; *wae*, sorrowful; *thole*, endure; *snash*, abuse; *poind*, seize; *'s ane*, as one; *poortith*, poverty.

Then chance and fortune are sae guided.
They're ay in less or mair provided;
An' tho' fatigu'd wi' close employment,
A blink o' rest's a sweet enjoyment.

The dearest comfort o' their lives,
Their grushie weans an' faithfu' wives;
The prattling things are just their pride,
That sweetens a' their fire side.

An' whyles twalpennie-worth o' nappy
Can mak the bodies unco happy;
They lay aside their private cares,
To mind the Kirk and State affairs;
They'll talk o' patronage an' priests,
Wi' kindling fury i' their breasts,
Or tell what new taxation's comin,
An' ferlie at the folk in Lon'on.

As bleak-fac'd Hallowmass returns,
They get the jovial, rantan Kirns,
When rural life, of ev'ry station,
Unite in common recreation;
Love blinks, Wit slaps, an' social Mirth
Forgets there's care upo' the earth.

That merry day the year begins,
They bar the door on frosty win's;
The nappy reeks wi' mantling ream,
An' sheds a heart-inspiring steam;
The luntan pipe, an' sneeshin mill,
Are handed round wi' right guid will;
The cantie, auld folks, crackan crouse,
The young anes rantan thro' the house —

grushie, thriving; *weans*, children; *nappy*, ale; *unco*, very; *ferlie*, wonder;
Kirns, harvest homes; *blinks*, winks; *win's*, winds; *reeks*, smokes; *ream*,
froth; *luntan*, smoking; *sneeshin-mill*, snuff box; *cantie*, cheerful; *crackin
crouse*, chatting happily; *rantan*, romping.

My heart has been sae fain to see them,
That I for joy hae barket wi' them.

    Still it's owre true that ye hae said,
Sic game is now owre aften play'd;
There's monie a creditable flock
O' decent, honest, fawsont folk,
Are riven out baith root an' branch,
Some rascal's pridefu' greed to quench,
Wha thinks to knit himsel the faster
In favor wi' some gentle Master,
Wha aiblins thrang a-parliamentin,
For Britain's guid his saul indentin —

CAESAR

Haith lad ye little ken about it;
For Britain's guid! guid faith! I doubt it.
Say rather, gaun as Premiers lead him,
An' saying *aye* or *no*'s they bid him:
At Operas an' Plays parading,
Mortgaging, gambling, masquerading:
Or maybe, in a frolic daft,
To Hague or Calais takes a waft,
To make a tour an' tak a whirl,
To learn *bon ton* and see the worl'.

    There, at Vienna or Versailles,
He rives his father's auld entails;
Or by Madrid he takes the rout,
To thrum guittars an' fecht wi' nowt;
Or down Italian vista startles,
Whore-hunting amang groves o' myrtles:

barket, barked; *fawsont*, seemly; *riven*, torn; *aiblins*, perhaps; *thrang*, busy;
saul, soul; *haith*, faith!; *gaun*, going; *rives*, robs; *fecht*, fight; *nowt*, cattle.

Then bowses drumlie German-water,
To mak himsel look fair and fatter,
An' purge the bitter ga's an' cankers,
O' curst Venetian bores an' chancres.*

For Britain's guid ! for her destruction !
Wi' dissipation, feud an' faction !

LUATH

Hech man ! dear sirs ! is that the gate
They waste sae mony a braw estate !
Are we sae foughten and harass'd
For gear to gang that gate at last !

O would they stay aback frae courts,
An' please themsels wi' countra sports,
It wad for ev'ry ane be better,
The Laird, the Tenant, an' the Cotter !
For thae frank, rantan, ramblan billies,
Fient haet o' them's ill hearted fellows ;
Except for breakin o' their timmer,
Or speakin lightly o' their limmer,
Or shootin of a hare or moorcock,
The ne'er-a-bit they're ill to poor folk.

But will ye tell me, master Caesar,
Sure great folk's life's a life o' pleasure ?
Nae cauld nor hunger e'er can steer them,
The vera thought o't need na fear them.

bowses, boozes ; drumlie, muddy ; ga's, sores ; gate, way ; foughten, worried ;
gear, wealth ; rantan, roystering ; billies, chaps, Fient haet, devil a one ;
timmer, woods ; limmer, mistress ; steer, disturb ; fear, frighten.

* In the Edinburgh edition Burns changed this couplet to :
"An' clear the consequential sorrows,
Love-gifts of Carnival Signoras."

Lord man, were ye but whyles where I am,
The gentles ye wad neer envy them!

It's true, they need na starve or sweat,
Thro' winter's cauld, or summer's heat;
They've nae sair-wark to craze their banes,
An' fill auld-age wi' grips an' granes;
But human-bodies are sic fools,
For a' their colledges an' schools,
That when nae real ills perplex them,
They mak enow themsels to vex them;
An' ay the less they hae to sturt them,
In like proportion, less will hurt them.

A country fellow at the pleugh,
His acre's till'd, he's right eneugh;
A country girl at her wheel,
Her dizzen's done, she's unco weel;
But gentlemen, an' ladies warst,
Wi' ev'n down want o' wark are curst.
They loiter, lounging, lank an' lazy;
Tho' deil-haet ails them, yet uneasy;
Their days, insipid, dull an' tasteless,
Their nights, unquiet, lang an' restless.

An' ev'n their sports, their balls an' races,
Their galloping through public places,
There's sic parade, sic pomp an' art,
The joy can scarcely reach the heart.

The men cast out in party-matches,
Then sowther a' in deep debauches.
Ae night, they're mad wi' drink an' whuring,
Niest day their life is past enduring.

sair-wark, hard work; *banes*, bones; *grips*, gripes; *granes*, groans; *sturt*,
annoy; *pleugh*, plough; *dizzen*, dozen; *warst*, worst; *down*, utter, down-
right; *deil-haet*, devil the thing; *sowther*, solder; *Niest*, next.

The ladies arm-in-arm in clusters,
As great an' gracious a' as sisters;
But hear their absent thoughts o' ither,
They're a' run deils an' jads thegither.
Whyles, owre the wee bit cup an' platie,
They sip the scandal-potion pretty;
Or lee-lang nights, wi' crabbet leuks,
Pore owre the devil's pictur'd beuks;
Stake on a chance a farmer's stackyard,
An' cheat like ony unhang'd blackguard.

There's some exceptions, man an' woman;
But this is gentry's life in common.

By this, the sun was out o' sight,
An' darker gloamin brought the night:
The bum-clock humm'd wi' lazy drone,
The kye stood rowtan i' the loan;
When up they gat an' shook their lugs,
Rejoic'd they were na men but dogs;
An' each took off his several way,
Resolv'd to meet some ither day.

                                                    1786

ither, each other; *run*, downright; *jads*, jades; *lee-lang*, livelong; *crabbet leuks*, crabbed looks; *devil's ... beuks*, playing cards; *gloamin*, dusk; *bum-clock*, beetle; *kye*, cattle; *rowtan*, lowing; *loan*, lane; *gat*, got; *lugs*, ears.

Holy Willie's Prayer

And send the Godly in a pet to pray —
POPE

Argument

Holy Willie was a rather oldish bachelor Elder in the parish of Mauchline, & much & justly famed for that polemical chattering which ends in tippling Orthodoxy, & for that Spiritualised Bawdry which refines to Liquorish Devotion. — In a Sessional process with a gentleman in Mauchline, a Mr Gavin Hamilton,* Holy Willie, & his priest, father Auld, after full hearing in the Presbytery of Ayr, came off but second best; owing partly to the oratorical powers of Mr Robt Aiken, Mr Hamilton's Counsel; but chiefly to Mr Hamilton's being one of the most irreproachable & truly respectable characters in the country. On losing his Process, the Muse overheard him at his devotions as follows —

O thou that in the heavens does dwell!
Wha, as it pleases best thysel,
Sends ane to heaven & ten to hell,
                    A' for thy glory!
And no for ony gude or ill
                    They've done before thee.

I bless & praise thy matchless might,
When thousands thou has left in night,
That I am here before thy sight,
                    For gifts & grace,
A burning & a shining light
                    To a' this place.

What was I, or my generation,
That I should get such exaltation?

---

* Hamilton, dedicatee of the Kilmarnock edition, a lawyer in Mauchline, liberal in his views and persecuted by the Kirk Session of Mauchline at the hands of the Rev. William Auld, subject of these verses. (Ed.)

I, wha deserv'd most just damnation,
                    For broken laws
Sax thousand years ere my creation,
                    Thro' Adam's cause.

When from my mother's womb I fell,
Thou might hae plunged me deep in hell,
To gnash my gooms, & weep, & wail,
                    In burning lakes,
Where damned devils roar & yell
                    Chain'd to their stakes.

Yet I am here, a chosen sample,
To shew thy grace is great & ample:
I'm here, a pillar o' thy temple
                    Strong as a rock,
A guide, a ruler & example
                    To a' thy flock.

But yet — O Lord — confess I must —
At times I'm fash'd wi' fleshly lust;
And sometimes too, in warldly trust
                    Vile Self gets in;
But thou remembers we are dust,
                    Defil'd wi' sin.

O Lord — yestreen — thou kens — wi' Meg —
Thy pardon I sincerely beg!
O may't ne'er be a living plague,
                    To my dishonor!
And I'll ne'er lift a lawless leg
                    Again upon her.

Besides, I farther maun avow,
Wi' Leezie's lass, three times — I trow —

gooms, gums; *fash'd*, troubled; *yestreen*, last night; *kens*, knowest; *maun*, must.

42

But, Lord, that friday I was fou
                    When I cam near her;
Or else, thou kens, thy servant true
                    Wad never steer her.

Maybe thou lets this fleshly thorn
Buffet thy servant e'en & morn,
Lest he o'er proud & high should turn,
                    That he's sae gifted;
If sae, thy hand maun e'en be borne
                    Untill thou lift it.

Lord bless thy Chosen in this place,
For here thou has a chosen race:
But God, confound their stubborn face,
                    And blast their name,
Wha bring thy rulers to disgrace
                    And open shame.

Lord mind Gaun Hamilton's deserts!
He drinks, & swears, & plays at cartes,
Yet has sae mony taking arts
                    Wi' great & sma',
Frae God's ain priest the people's hearts
                    He steals awa.

And when we chasten'd him therefore,
Thou kens how he bred sic a splore,
And set the warld in a roar
                    O' laughin at us:
Curse thou his basket and his store,
                    Kail & potatoes.

Lord hear my earnest cry & prayer
Against that Presbytry of Ayr!

wad, would; *steer*, meddle with; *sae*, so; *rulers*, elders; *mind*, remember;
cartes, cards; *ain*, own; *splore*, fuss; *Kail*, cabbage.

Thy strong right hand, Lord, make it bare
                    Upon their heads!
Lord visit them, & dinna spare,
                    For their misdeeds!

O Lord my God, that glib-tongu'd Aiken!*
My very heart & flesh are quaking
To think how I sat, sweating, shaking,
                    And piss'd wi' dread,
While Auld wi' hingin lip gaed sneaking
                    And hid his head!

Lord, in thy day o' vengeance try him!
Lord, visit him that did employ him!
And pass not in thy mercy by them;
                    Nor hear their prayer;
But for thy people's sake destroy them,
                    And dinna spare!

But Lord; remember me & mine
Wi' mercies temporal & divine!
That I for grace & gear may shine,
                    Excell'd by nane!
And a' the glory shall be thine!
                    Amen! Amen!

1785

hingin, hanging; *gaed*, went; *gear*, wealth.

* Robert Aiken, a convivial lawyer friend of Burns's, who defended Gavin Hamilton before the Presbytery of Ayr when charged with non-observance of the Sabbath and other wickednesses. Aiken was a great supporter of the poet ("my first kind patron") and collected nearly 150 subscriptions for the Kilmarnock edition. (Ed.)

Epistle to the Rev. John M'Math*

INCLOSING A COPY OF "HOLY WILLIE'S PRAYER", WHICH
HE HAD REQUESTED

Sept. 17, 1785

While at the stook the shearers cow'r
To shun the bitter blaudin show'r,
Or in gulravage rinnin scowr
   To pass the time,
To you I dedicate the hour
   In idle rhyme.

My musie, tir'd wi' mony a sonnet
On gown, an' ban', an' douce black bonnet,
Is grown right eerie now she's done it,
   Lest they should blame her,
An' rouse their holy thunder on it
   And anathem her.

I own 'twas rash, an' rather hardy,
That I a simple, country bardie,
Should meddle wi' a pack sae sturdy,
   Wha, if they ken me,
Can easy, wi' a single wordie,
   Lowse hell upon me.

But I gae mad at their grimaces,
Their sighin, cantin, grace-proud faces,
Their three-mile prayers, an' hauf-mile graces,
   Their raxin conscience,
Whase greed, revenge, an' pride disgraces
   Waur nor their nonsense.

While . . . , stooking corn; *shearers*, reapers; *blaudin*, pelting; *in gulravage rinnin scowr*, rush about the place having fun; *ban'*, white neck-bands of a minister; *douce*, respectable; *eerie*, fearful; *Lowse*, loose; *gae*, go; *raxin*, elastic; *Waur nor*, worse than.

 * A liberal-minded minister at Tarbolton. He supported Gavin Hamilton in his feud with the Kirk. (Ed.)

There's Gaw'n, misca'd waur than a beast,
Wha has mair honour in his breast
Than mony scores as guid's the priest
                    Wha sae abus'd him:
And may a bard no crack his jest
                    What way they've us'd him?

See him, the poor man's friend in need,
The gentleman in word an' deed —
An' shall his fame an' honour bleed
                    By worthless skellums,
An' not a muse erect her head
                    To cowe the blellums?

O Pope, had I thy satire's darts
To gie the rascals their deserts,
I'd rip their rotten, hollow hearts,
                    An' tell aloud
Their jugglin hocus-pocus arts
                    To cheat the crowd.

God knows, I'm no the thing I should be,
Nor am I even the thing I could be,
But twenty times I rather would be
                    An atheist clean,
Than under gospel colours hid be
                    Just for a screen.

An honest man may like a glass,
An honest man may like a lass,
But mean revenge, and malice fause
                    He'll still disdain,
An' then cry zeal for gospel laws,
                    Like some we ken.

Gaw'n, Gavin Hamilton (see note to "Holy Willie's Prayer"); *misca'd*,
abused; *what wey*, however; *skellums*, rogues; *cowe*, scare; *blellums*,
braggarts; *fause*, false.

46

They take religion in their mouth;
They talk o' mercy, grace an' truth,
For what? — to gie their malice skouth
     On some puir wight,
An' hunt him down, owre right and ruth,
     To ruin streight.

All hail, Religion! maid divine!
Pardon a muse sae mean as mine,
Wha in her rough imperfect line
     Thus daurs to name thee;
To stigmatise false friends of thine
     Can ne'er defame thee.

Tho' blotch't and foul wi' mony a stain,
An' far unworthy of thy train,
With trembling voice I tune my strain,
     To join with those
Who boldly dare thy cause maintain
     In spite of foes:

In spite o' crowds, in spite o' mobs,
In spite o' undermining jobs,
In spite o' dark banditti stabs
     At worth an' merit,
By scoundrels, even wi' holy robes,
     But hellish spirit.

O Ayr! my dear, my native ground,
Within thy presbyterial bound
A candid liberal band is found
     Of public teachers,
As men, as Christians too, renown'd,
     An' manly preachers.

  skouth, scope; *puir*, poor; *daurs*, dares.

Sir, in that circle you are nam'd;
Sir, in that circle you are fam'd;
An' some, by whom your doctrine's blam'd
               (Which gie's you honour)
Even, sir, by them your heart's esteem'd,
               An' winning manner.

Pardon this freedom I have ta'en,
An' if impertinent I've been,
Impute it not, good sir, in ane
               Whase heart ne'er wrang'd ye,
But to his utmost would befriend
               Ought that belang'd ye.

belang'd, belonged to.

Address to the Deil

O Prince! O Chief of many throned Powr's,
That led th' embattl'd Seraphim to war —
                         MILTON

O Thou! whatever title suit thee,
Auld Hornie, Satan, Nick, or Clootie,
Wha in yon cavern grim an' sootie,
               Clos'd under hatches,
Spairges about the brunstane cootie
               To scaud poor wretches!

Hear me, auld Hangie, for a wee,
An' let poor, damned bodies be;
I'm sure sma' pleasure it can gie,
               Ev'n to a deil,
To skelp an' scaud poor dogs like me,
               An' hear us squeel!

Clootie, Cloven-Foot; *Spairges*, splashes; *brunstane*, brimstone; *cootie*, bowl; *scaud*, scald; *Hangie*, hangman; *skelp*, slap.

Great is thy pow'r, an' great thy fame;
Far kend an' noted is thy name;
An' tho' yon lowin heugh's thy hame,
          Thou travels far;
An' faith! thou's neither lag nor lame,
             Nor blate nor scaur.

Whyles, ranging like a roarin lion,
For prey, a' holes an' corners tryin;
Whyles, on the strong-wing'd tempest flyin,
          Tirlin the kirks;
Whyles, in the human bosom pryin,
             Unseen thou lurks.

I've heard my reverend Graunie say,
In lanely glens ye like to stray;
Or where auld, ruin'd castles, gray,
          Nod to the moon,
Ye fright the nightly wand'rer's way,
             Wi' eldritch croon.

When twilight did my Graunie summon,
To say her pray'rs, douce, honest woman!
Aft yont the dyke she's heard you bummin,
          Wi' eerie drone;
Or, rustlin, thro' the boortries comin,
             Wi' heavy groan.

Ae dreary, windy, winter night,
The stars shot down wi' sklentin light,
Wi' you, mysel, I gat a fright,
          Ayont the lough;
Ye, like a rash-buss, stood in sight,
             Wi' waving sugh.

---

lowin heugh, flaming pit; *lag,* backward; *blate,* bashful; *scaur,* scared; *Whyles,* sometimes; *Tirlin,* unroofing; *lanely,* lonely; *douce,* decent; *yont,* beyond; *bummin,* humming; *boortries,* elder trees; *sklentin,* slanting; *Ayont,* beyond; *lough,* pond; *rash-buss,* clump of rushes; *sugh,* soughing.

The cudgel in my nieve did shake,
Each bristl'd hair stood like a stake,
When wi' an eldritch, stoor quaick, quaick,
        Amang the springs,
Awa ye squatter'd like a drake,
        On whistling wings.

Let warlocks grim, an' wither'd hags,
Tell how wi' you on ragweed nags,
They skim the muirs an' dizzy crags,
        Wi' wicked speed;
And in kirk-yards renew their leagues,
        Owre howkit dead.

Thence, countra wives, wi' toil an' pain,
May plunge an' plunge the kirn in vain;
For, Oh! the yellow treasure's taen
        By witching skill;
An' dawtit, twal-pint Hawkie's gaen
        As yell's the bill.

Thence, mystic knots mak great abuse,
On young guidmen, fond, keen, an' crouse;
When the best wark-lume i' the house,
        By cantraip wit,
Is instant made no worth a louse,
        Just at the bit.

When thowes dissolve the snawy hoord,
An' float the jinglin icy-boord,
Then, water-kelpies haunt the foord,
        By your direction,
An' nighted trav'llers are allur'd
        To their destruction.

nieve, fist; *stoor*, hoarse; *squattered*, fluttered; *ragweed*, broomstick;
howkit, dug up; *countra*, country; *kirn*, churn; *dawtit*, petted; *twal-pint*,
twelve-pint; *Hawkie*, cow; *gaen*, gone; *yell*, dry; *bill*, bull; *guidmen*,
husbands; *crouse*, confident; *wark-lume*, tool; *cantraip*, magic; *at the bit*,
when needed; *thowes*, thaws; *hoord*, hoard; *boord*, surface.

An' aft your moss-traversing spunkies
Decoy the wight that late an' drunk is:
The bleezin, curst, mischievous monkies
        Delude his eyes;
Till in some miry slough he sunk is
        Ne'er mair to rise.

When Masons' mystic word an' grip,
In storms an' tempests raise you up,
Some cock or cat your rage maun stop,
        Or, strange to tell!
The youngest Brother ye wad whip
        Aff straught to hell.

Lang syne in Eden's bonie yard,
When youthfu' lovers first were pair'd,
An' all the Soul of Love they shar'd,
        The raptur'd hour,
Sweet on the fragrant, flow'ry swaird,
        In shady bow'r:

Then you, ye auld, snick-drawing dog!
Ye cam to Paradise incog.
An' play'd on man a cursed brogue,
        (Black be your fa'!)
An' gied the infant warld a shog,
        'Maist ruin'd a'.

D'ye mind that day, when in a bizz,
Wi' reekit duds, an' reestit gizz,
Ye did present your smoutie phiz,
        'Mang better folk,
An' sklented on the man of Uzz
        Your spitefu' joke?

moss, bog; *spunkies*, will-o'-the-wisps; *bleezin*, blazing; *mair*, more;
maun, must; *straught*, straight; *Lang syne*, long ago; *yard*, garden; *swaird*,
sward; *snick-drawing*, stealthy (latch-lifting); *brogue*, trick; *fa'*, fall; *gied*,
gave; *shog*, shake; *'Maist*, almost; *bizz*, bustle; *reekit*, smoky; *duds*,
clothes; *reestit gizz*, scorched wig; *smoutie*, smutty; *sklented*, cast.

An' how ye gat him i' your thrall,
An' brak him out o' house an' hal',
While scabs an' botches did him gall,
   Wi' bitter claw,
An' lows'd his ill-tongu'd, wicked Scawl,
   Was warst ava?

But a' your doings to rehearse,
Your wily snares an' fechtin fierce,
Sin' that day Michael* did you pierce,
   Down to this time,
Wad ding a Lallan tongue, or Erse,
   In prose or rhyme.

An' now, auld Cloots, I ken ye're thinkin,
A certain Bardie's rantin, drinkin,
Some luckless hour will send him linkin
   To your black pit;
But, faith! he'll turn a corner jinkin,
   An' cheat you yet.

But fare you weel, auld Nickie-ben!
O wad ye tak a thought an' men'!
Ye aiblins might — I dinna ken —
   Still hae a stake —
I'm wae to think upo' yon den,
   Ev'n for your sake!

          1785

lows'd, loosed; *Scawl*, scold; *warst*, worst; *ava*, of all; *fechtin*, fighting; *ding*, beat; *Lallan*, Lowland; *rantin*, roistering; *linkin*, hurrying; *jinkin*, dodging; *men'*, mend; *aiblins*, perhaps; *stake*, chance; *wae*, sad.

   * *vide* Milton, Book V. (Burns's note.)

Death and Doctor Hornbook*

Some books are lies frae end to end,
And some great lies were never penn'd:
Ev'n Ministers they hae been kenn'd,
      In holy rapture,
A rousing whid, at times, to vend,
        And nail't wi' Scripture.

But this that I am gaun to tell,
Which lately on a night befel,
Is just as true's the Deil's in hell
      Or Dublin city:
That e'er he nearer comes oursel
        'S a muckle pity.

The clachan yill had made me canty,
I was na fou, but just had plenty;
I stacher'd whyles, but yet took tent ay
      To free the ditches;
An' hillocks, stanes an' bushes kenn'd ay
        Frae ghaists an' witches.

The rising moon began to glowr
The distant Cumnock hills out-owre:
To count her horns, wi' a' my pow'r
      I set mysel;
But whether she had three or four,
        I cou'd na tell.

kenn'd, known; *whid*, lie; *vend*, vent; *gaun*, going; *muckle*, great; *clachan yill*, village ale; *canty*, jolly; *fou*, drunk; *stacher'd*, staggered, *whyles*, now and then; *took tent*, took care; *free*, clear; *kenn'd*, known; *out-owre*, away over.

   * John Wilson, schoolmaster at Tarbolton. He opened a grocery shop to supplement his poor wage and sold medicines and gave medical advice gratis. He evidently took the satire in good part. (Ed.)

I was come round about the hill,
And todlin down on Willie's mill,
Setting my staff wi' a' my skill,
                    To keep me sicker;
Tho' leeward whyles, against my will,
                    I took a bicker.

I there wi' *Something* does forgather,
That pat me in an eerie swither;
An awfu' scythe, out-owre ae shouther,
                    Clear-dangling, hang;
A three-tae'd leister on the ither
                    Lay, large an' lang.

Its stature seem'd lang Scotch ells twa,
The queerest shape that e'er I saw,
For fient a wame it had ava;
                    And then its shanks,
They were as thin, as sharp an' sma'
                    As cheeks o' branks.

"Guid-een" quo' I; "Friend! hae ye been mawin,
When ither folk are busy sawin?"*
It seem'd to mak a kind o' stan',
                    But naething spak;
At length, says I, "Friend, whare ye gaun,
                    Will ye go back?"

It spak right howe — "My name is Death,
But be na' fley'd." — Quoth I, "Guid faith,

sicker, steady; *whyles*, at times; *bicker*, run; *forgather*, meet; *pat*, put;
swither, doubt; *out-owre ae shouther*, over one shoulder; *three-taed leister*,
trident; *fient*, devil; *wame*, belly; *ava*, at all; *cheeks*, sides; *branks*, wooden
bridle; *mawin*, mowing; *sawin*, sowing; *stan'*, stand; *spak*, spoke;
whare . . . , where are you going; *howe*, hollow; *fley'd*, scared.

* This rencounter happened in seed-time, 1785. (Burns's note.)

Ye're maybe come to stap my breath;
            But tent me, billie;
I red ye weel, tak care o' skaith,
            See, there's a gully!"

"Gudeman," quo' he, "put up your whittle,
I'm no design'd to try its mettle;
But if I did, I wad be kittle
            To be mislear'd,
I wad na mind it, no that spittle
            Out-owre my beard."

"Weel, weel!" says I, "a bargain be't;
Come, gie's your hand, an' sae we're gree't:
We'll ease our shanks an' tak a seat,
            Come, gie's your news;
This while* ye hae been mony a gate,
            At mony a house."

"Ay, ay!" quo' he, an' shook his head,
"It's e'en a lang, lang time indeed
Sin I began to nick the thread,
            An' choke the breath:
Folk maun do something for their bread,
            An' sae maun Death.

"Sax thousand years are near hand fled
Sin' I was to the butching bred,
An' mony a scheme in vain's been laid,
            To stap or scar me;
Till ane Hornbook's† ta'en up the trade,
            an' faith, he'll waur me.

tent, heed; *billie*, fellow; *red*, advise; *scaith*, harm; *gully*, large knife;
whittle, blade; *design'd*, intending; *kittle*, smart; *mislear'd*, unmannerly,
mischievous; *spittle*, spit; *gree't*, agreed; *gate*, road; *nick*, cut; *maun*, must;
near hand, well-nigh; *stap or scar*, stop or scare; *waur*, worst.

* An epidemical fever was then raging in that country. (Burns's note.)
† This gentleman, Dr. Hornbook, is, professionally, a brother of the
sovereign Order of the Ferula; but, by intuition and inspiration, is at
once an Apothecary, Surgeon, and Physician. (Burns's note.)

"Ye ken Jock Hornbook i' the clachan,
Deil mak his king's-hood in a spleuchan!
He's grown sae weel acquaint wi' Buchan,*
        And ither chaps,
The weans haud out their fingers laughin,
        An' pouk my hips.

"See, here's a scythe, an' there's a dart,
They hae pierc'd mony a gallant heart;
But Doctor Hornbook, wi' his art
        And cursed skill,
Has made them baith no worth a fart,
        Damn'd haet they'll kill!

" 'Twas but yestreen, nae farther gaen,
I threw a noble throw at ane;
Wi' less, I'm sure, I've hundreds slain;
        But deil-ma-care!
It just play'd dirl on the bane,
        But did nae mair.

"Hornbook was by, wi' ready art,
An' had sae fortify'd the part,
That when I looked to my dart,
        It was sae blunt,
Fient haet o't wad hae pierc'd the heart
        Of a kail-runt.

"I drew my scythe in sic a fury,
I nearhand cowpit wi' my hurry,
But yet the bauld Apothecary
        Withstood the shock;
I might as weel hae try'd a quarry
        O' hard whin-rock.

clachan, village; *king's-hood*, scrotum; *spleuchan*, tobacco-pouch; *weans*, children; *haud*, hold; *pouk*, poke; *baith*, both; *Damn'd haet*, the devil a one; *gaen*, gone; *dirl*, rattle; *bane*, bone; *nae mair*, no more; *Fient haet*, Devil a bit; *kail-runt*, cabbage stalk; *sic*, such; *nearhand cowpit*, almost tumbled.

* Buchan's Domestic Medicine. (Burns's note.)

"Ev'n them he canna get attended,
Altho' their face he ne'er had kend it,
Just shit in a kail-blade and send it,
   As soon's he smells't,
Baith their disease, and what will mend it,
   At once he tells't.

"And then a' doctor's saws and whittles,
Of a' dimensions, shapes, an' mettles,
A' kinds o' boxes, mugs an' bottles,
   He's sure to hae;
Their Latin names as fast he rattles
   As A B C.

"Calces o' fossils, earth, and trees;
True Sal-marinum o' the seas;
The Farina of beans and pease,
   He has't in plenty;
Aqua-fontis, what you please,
   He can content ye.

"Forbye some new, uncommon weapons,
Urinus Spiritus of capons;
Or Mite-horn shavings, filings, scrapings,
   Distill'd *per se*;
Sal-alkali o' Midge-tail-clippings,
   And mony mae."

"Waes me for Johnny Ged's Hole* now,"
Quoth I, "if that thae news be true!
His braw calf-ward whare gowans grew,
   Sae white and bonie,
Nae doubt they'll rive it wi' the plew;
   They'll ruin Johnie!"

kend, known; *kail-blade*, cabbage leaf; *whittles*, knives; *Forbye*, besides; *mony mae*, many more; *thae*, these; *braw calf-ward*, fine pasture; *gowans*, daisies; *rive*, break up; *plew*, plough.

* The grave-digger. (Burns's note.)

The creature grain'd an eldritch laugh,
And says "Ye needna yoke the pleugh,
Kirk-yards will soon be till'd eneugh,
      Tak ye nae fear:
They'll a' be trench'd wi mony a sheugh,
      In twa-three year.

"Whare I kill'd ane, a fair strae-death,
By loss o' blood, or want o' breath,
This night I'm free to tak my aith,
      That Hornbook's skill
Has clad a score i' their last claith,
      By drap and pill.

"An honest Wabster to his trade,
Whase wife's twa nieves were scarce weel-bred,
Gat tippence-worth to mend her head,
      When it was sair;
The wife slade cannie to her bed,
      But ne'er spak mair.

"A countra Laird had ta'en the batts,
Or some curmurring in his guts,
His only son for Hornbook sets,
      An' pays him well.
The lad, for twa guid gimmer-pets,
      Was Laird himsel.

"A bonie lass, ye kend her name,
Some ill-brewn drink had hov'd her wame;

grain'd, groaned; *eldritch*, weird; *sheugh*, ditch; *strae-death*, natural death in bed; *aith*, oath; *claith*, cloth; *drap*, drop; *Wabster*, weaver; *nieves*, fists; *sair*, aching; *slade cannie*, crept quietly; *batts*, colic; *curmurring*, rumbling; *sets*, sets out; *gimmer-pets*, pet ewes; *hov'd her wame*, swelled her belly.

She trusts hersel, to hide the shame,
                    In Hornbook's care;
Horn sent her aff to her lang hame,
                    To hide it there.

"That's just a swatch o' Hornbook's way,
Thus goes he on from day to day,
Thus does he poison, kill, an' slay,
                    An's weel paid for't;
Yet stops me o' my lawfu' prey,
                    Wi' his damn'd dirt!

"But hark! I'll tell you of a plot,
Tho' dinna ye be speakin o't;
I'll nail the self-conceited Sot,
                    As dead's a herrin;
Niest time we meet, I'll wad a groat,
                    He gets his fairin!"

But just as he began to tell,
The auld kirk-hammer strak the bell
Some wee short hour ayont the twal,
                    Which rais'd us baith;
I took the way that pleas'd mysel,
                    And sae did Death.

1785

lang hame, long home (paradise); *swatch*, sample; *Niest*, next; *wad*, bet;
fairin, deserts; *strak*, struck; *ayont the twal*, after midnight; *rais'd*, roused;
baith, both.

Tam o' Shanter

A TALE

Of Brownyis and of Bogillis full is this buke.
GAWIN DOUGLAS

When chapman billies leave the street,
And drouthy neebors, neebors meet,
As market-days are wearing late,
An' folk begin to tak the gate;
While we sit bousing at the nappy,
An' getting fou and unco happy,
We think na on the lang Scots miles,
The mosses, waters, slaps, and styles,
That lie between us and our hame,
Whare sits our sulky sullen dame,
Gathering her brows like gathering storm,
Nursing her wrath to keep it warm.

This truth fand honest Tam o' Shanter,
As he frae Ayr ae night did canter,
(Auld Ayr, wham ne'er a town surpasses,
For honest men and bonny lasses).

O Tam! had'st thou but been sae wise,
As ta'en thy ain wife Kate's advice!
She tauld thee weel thou was a skellum,
A blethering, blustering, a drunken blellum;
That frae November till October,
Ae market-day thou was nae sober;
That ilka melder, wi' the miller,
Thou sat as lang as thou had siller;

chapman billies, packman fellows; *drouthy*, thirsty; *neebors*, neighbours;
gate, road; *nappy*, ale; *fou*, drunk; *unco*, extra; *na*, not; *moss*, bog; *slaps*,
gaps in walls; *fand*, found; *ta'en*, taken; *ain*, own; *skellum*, rogue;
blethering, chattering; *blellum*, boaster; *ilka melder*, every meal-grinding;
siller, money.

That ev'ry naig was ca'ed a shoe on,
The smith and thee got roaring fou on;
That at the Lord's house, even on Sunday,
Thou drank wi' Kirkton Jean till Monday.
She prophesied that, late or soon,
Thou would be found deep drown'd in Doon;
Or catch'd wi' warlocks in the mirk,
By Alloway's auld haunted kirk.

    Ah, gentle dames! it gars me greet,
To think how mony counsels sweet,
How mony lengthen'd sage advices,
The husband frae the wife despises!

    But to our tale: Ae market-night,
Tam had got planted unco right;
Fast by an ingle, bleezing finely,
Wi' reaming swats, that drank divinely;
And at his elbow, Souter Johnny,
His ancient, trusty, drouthy crony;
Tam lo'ed him like a vera brither;
They had been fou for weeks thegither.
The night drave on wi' sangs and clatter;
And ay the ale was growing better:
The landlady and Tam grew gracious,
Wi' favours, secret, sweet, and precious:
The Souter tauld his queerest stories;
The landlord's laugh was ready chorus:
The storm without might rair and rustle,
Tam did na mind the storm a whistle.

    Care, mad to see a man sae happy,
E'en drown'd himsel amang the nappy:

ev'ry naig was ca'ed a shoe on, every horse shoed; *gars*, makes; *greet*, weep;
Ae, one; *bleezing*, blazing; *reaming swats*, frothing ale; *Souter*, cobbler;
drouthy, thirsty; *lo'ed*, loved; *thegither*, together; *drave*, drove; *clatter*,
gossip; *rair*, roar; *nappy*, drink.

As bees flee hame wi' lades o' treasure,
The minutes wing'd their way wi' pleasure:
Kings may be blest, but Tam was glorious,
O'er a' the ills o' life victorious!

But pleasures are like poppies spread,
You sieze the flow'r, its bloom is shed;
Or like the snow falls in the river,
A moment white — then melts for ever;
Or like the borealis race,
That flit ere you can point their place;
Or like the rainbow's lovely form
Evanishing amid the storm. —
Nae man can tether time or tide;
The hour approaches Tam maun ride;
That hour, o' night's black arch the key-stane,
That dreary hour he mounts his beast in;
And sic a night he taks the road in,
As ne'er poor sinner was abroad in.

The wind blew as 'twad blawn its last;
The rattling showers rose on the blast;
The speedy gleams the darkness swallow'd;
Loud, deep, and lang, the thunder bellow'd:
That night, a child might understand,
The Deil had business on his hand.

Weel mounted on his gray mare, Meg,
A better never lifted leg,
Tam skelpit on thro' dub and mire,
Despising wind, and rain, and fire;
Whiles holding fast his gude blue bonnet;
Whiles crooning o'er some auld Scots sonnet;
Whiles glowring round wi' prudent cares,
Lest bogles catch him unawares:

lades, loads; 'twad . . . , as if it would have blown; skelpit, dashed; dub,
puddle; Whiles, now; sonnet, song; glowring, staring; bogles, bogies.

Kirk-Alloway was drawing nigh,
Whare ghaists and houlets nightly cry. —

By this time he was cross the ford,
Whare, in the snaw, the chapman smoor'd;
And past the birks and meikle stane,
Whare drunken Charlie brak's neck-bane;
And thro' the whins, and by the cairn,
Whare hunters fand the murder'd bairn;
And near the thorn, aboon the well,
Whare Mungo's mither hang'd hersel. —
Before him Doon pours all his floods;
The doubling storm roars thro' the woods;
The lightnings flash from pole to pole;
Near and more near the thunders roll:
When, glimmering thro' the groaning trees,
Kirk-Alloway seem'd in a bleeze;
Thro' ilka bore the beams were glancing;
And loud resounded mirth and dancing. —

Inspiring bold John Barleycorn!
What dangers thou can make us scorn!
Wi' tippeny, we fear nae evil;
Wi' usquabae, we'll face the devil! —
The swats sae ream'd in Tammy's noddle,
Fair play, he car'd na deils a boddle.
But Maggie stood right sair astonish'd,
Till, by the heel and hand admonish'd,
She ventur'd forward on the light;
And, wow! Tam saw an unco sight!
Warlocks and witches in a dance;
Nae cotillion, brent new frae France,
But hornpipes, jigs, strathspeys, and reels,
Put life and mettle in their heels.

ghaists, ghosts; *houlets*, owls; *smoor'd*, smothered; *birks*, birches; *whins*,
furze; *bore*, chink; *tippeny*, ale; *usquabae*, whisky; *boddle*, farthing; *brent*,
brand.

A winnock-bunker in the east,
There sat auld Nick, in shape o' beast;
A towzie tyke, black, grim, and large,
To gie them music was his charge:
He screw'd the pipes and gart them skirl,
Till roof and rafters a' did dirl. —
Coffins stood round, like open presses,
That shaw'd the dead in their last dresses;
And by some devilish cantraip slight
Each in its cauld hand held a light. —
By which heroic Tam was able
To note upon the haly table,
A murderer's banes in gibbet airns;
Twa span-lang, unchristen'd bairns;
A thief, new-cutted frae a rape,
Wi' his last gasp his gab did gape;
Five tomahawks, wi' blude red-rusted;
Five scymitars, wi' murder crusted;*
A garter, which a babe had strangled;
A knife, a father's throat had mangled,
Whom his ain son o' life bereft,
The grey hairs yet stack to the heft;
Wi' mair o' horrible and awefu',
Which even to name wad be unlawfu'.†

As Tammie glower'd, amaz'd, and curious,
The mirth and fun grew fast and furious:

winnock-bunker, window-seat; *towzie tyke*, shaggy dog; *gart*, made; *dirl*,
rattle; *cantraip slight*, weird trick; *haly*, holy; *airns*, irons; *rape*, rope.

* In one MS, after this line the following couplet occurs, deleted:
    "Seven gallows pins; three hangman's whittles (knives);
    A raw (row) of weel seal'd Doctor's bottles.' (Ed.)

† Burns was persuaded to omit the following lines here:
    "Three Lawyers' tongues, turn'd inside out,
    Wi' lies seam'd like a beggar's clout (coat);
    Three Priests' hearts, rotten, black as muck,
    Lay stinking, vile, in every neuk (corner)." (Ed.)

The piper loud and louder blew;
The dancers quick and quicker flew;
They reel'd, they set, they cross'd, they cleekit,
Till ilka carlin swat and reekit,
And coost her duddies to the wark,
And linket at it in her sark!

Now, Tam, O Tam! had thae been queans,
A' plump and strapping in their teens,
Their sarks, instead o' creeshie flannen,
Been snaw-white seventeen hunder linnen!*
Thir breeks o' mine, my only pair,
That ance were plush, o' gude blue hair,
I wad hae gi'en them off my hurdies,
For ae blink o' the bonie burdies!

But wither'd beldams, auld and droll,
Rigwoodie hags wad spean a foal,
Lowping and flinging on a crummock,
I wonder didna turn thy stomach.

But Tam kend what was what fu' brawlie,
There was ae winsome wench and wawlie,
That night enlisted in the core,
(Lang after kend on Carrick shore;
For mony a beast to dead she shot,
And perish'd mony a bony boat,
And shook baith meikle corn and bear,
And kept the country-side in fear).
Her cutty sark, o' Paisley harn,
That while a lassie she had worn,

cleekit, joined hands; *carlin*, witch; *swat an' reekit*, sweated and steamed; *coost*, cast off; *duddies*, rags; *linket*, tripped; *sark*, shift; *thae*, those; *queans*, girls; *creeshie*, greasy; *Thir*, these; *ance*, once; *hurdies*, buttocks; *ae blink*, one glimpse; *Rigwoodie*, scraggy; *spean*, wean; *Lowping*, leaping; *crummock*, staff; *brawlie*, well; *wawlie*, choice; *core*, company; *baith*, both; *meikle*, much; *bear*, barley; *cutty sark*, short shift; *harn*, coarse cloth.

* Woven in a reed of 1700 divisions. (Ed.)

In longitude tho' sorely scanty,
It was her best, and she was vauntie. —
Ah! little kend thy reverend grannie,
That sark she coft for her wee Nannie,
Wi' twa pund Scots ('twas a' her riches),
Wad ever grac'd a dance of witches!

But here my Muse her wing maun cour;
Sic flights are far beyond her pow'r;
To sing how Nannie lap and flang,
(A souple jade she was, and strang),
And how Tam stood, like ane bewitch'd,
And thought his very een enrich'd;
Even Satan glowr'd, and fidg'd fu' fain,
And hotch'd and blew wi' might and main:
Till first ae caper, syne anither,
Tam tint his reason a' thegither,
And roars out, "Weel done, Cutty-sark!"
And in an instant all was dark:
And scarcely had he Maggie rallied,
When out the hellish legion sallied.

As bees bizz out wi' angry fyke,
When plundering herds assail their byke;
As open pussie's mortal foes,
When, pop! she starts before their nose;
As eager runs the market-crowd,
When "Catch the thief!" resounds aloud;
So Maggie runs, the witches follow,
Wi' mony an eldritch skreech and hollow.

Ah, Tam! Ah, Tam! thou'll get thy fairin!
In hell they'll roast thee like a herrin!
In vain thy Kate awaits thy comin!
Kate soon will be a woefu' woman!

vauntie, proud; *coft*, bought; *pund*, pounds; *cour*, stoop; *lap and flang*,
leaped and kicked; *souple*, supple; *fidg'd fu' fain*, wriggled with delight;
hotch'd, jerked; *syne*, then; *tint*, lost; *fyke*, fret; *herds*, shepherds; *byke*,
hive; *pussie*, the hare; *eldritch skreech*, unearthly yell; *fairin*, deserts.

Now, do thy speedy utmost, Meg,
And win the key-stane* of the brig;
There at them thou thy tail may toss,
A running stream they dare na cross.
But ere the key-stane she could make,
The fient a tail she had to shake!
For Nannie, far before the rest,
Hard upon noble Maggie prest,
And flew at Tam wi' furious ettle;
But little wist she Maggie's mettle —
Ae spring brought off her master hale,
But left behind her ain grey tail:
The carlin claught her by the rump,
And left poor Maggie scarce a stump.

    Now, wha this tale o' truth shall read,
Ilk man and mother's son, take heed:
Whene'er to drink you are inclin'd,
Or cutty-sarks run in your mind,
Think, ye may buy the joys o'er dear,
Remember Tam o' Shanter's mare.

1790

fient, devil; *ettle*, intent; *hale*, whole; *claught*, clutched.

* It is a well-known fact that witches, or any evil spirits, have no power to follow a poor wight any farther than the middle of the next running stream. — It may be proper likewise to mention to the benighted traveller, that when he falls in with *bogles*, whatever danger may be in his going forward, there is much more hazard in turning back. (Burns's note.)

To a Mouse

ON TURNING HER UP IN HER NEST,
WITH THE PLOUGH, NOVEMBER 1785

Wee, sleekit, cowrin, tim'rous beastie,
O, what a panic's in thy breastie!
Thou need na start awa sae hasty,
    Wi' bickering brattle!
I wad be laith to rin an' chase thee,
    Wi' murd'ring pattle!

I'm truly sorry Man's dominion
Has broken Nature's social union,
An' justifies that ill opinion,
    Which makes thee startle,
At me, thy poor, earth-born companion,
    An' fellow-mortal!

I doubt na, whyles, but thou may thieve;
What then? poor beastie, thou maun live!
A daimen icker in a thrave
    'S a sma' request.
I'll get a blessin wi' the lave,
    An' never miss't!

Thy wee-bit housie, too, in ruin!
Its silly wa's the win's are strewin!
An' naething, now, to big a new ane,
    O' foggage green!
An' bleak December's winds ensuin,
    Baith snell an' keen!

---

sleekit, sleek; *bickering*, scrambling; *brattle*, clatter; *laith*, loth; *rin*, run; *pattle*, ploughstaff; *whyles*, sometimes; *daimen icker*, odd ear; *thrave*, twenty-four sheaves; *lave*, what's left; *silly*, feeble; *win's*, winds; *strewin* scattering; *big*, build; *foggage*, moss; *snell*, biting.

Thou saw the fields laid bare an' waste,
An' weary winter comin fast,
An' cozie here, beneath the blast,
                Thou thought to dwell,
Till crash! the cruel coulter past
                Out thro' thy cell.

That wee-bit heap o' leaves an' stibble
Has cost thee monie a weary nibble!
Now thou's turn'd out, for a' thy trouble,
                But house or hald,
To thole the Winter's sleety dribble,
                An' cranreuch cauld!

But, Mousie, thou art no thy lane,
In proving foresight may be vain:
The best-laid schemes o' mice an' men
                Gang aft a-gley,
An' lea'e us nought but grief an' pain,
                For promis'd joy!

Still thou art blest, compar'd wi' me!
The present only toucheth thee:
But, Och! I backward cast my e'e
                On prospects drear!
An' forward, tho' I canna see,
                I guess an' fear!

stibble, stubble; *but*, without; *hald*, holding; *thole*, endure; *cranreuch*, hoar-frost; *lane*, alone; *a-gley*, awry; *lea'e*, leave; *e'e*, eye.

A Winter Night (First Part only)

Poor naked wretches, wheresoe'er you are,
That bide the pelting of this pitiless storm!
How shall your houseless heads, and unfed sides,
Your loop'd and window'd raggedness, defend you
From seasons such as these?

SHAKESPEARE

When biting Boreas, fell and dour,
Sharp shivers thro' the leafless bow'r;
When Phoebus gies a short-liv'd glow'r,
        Far south the lift,
Dim-dark'ning thro' the flaky show'r,
          Or whirling drift:

Ae night the storm the steeples rockèd,
Poor Labour sweet in sleep was lockèd,
While burns, wi' snawy wreaths up-chokèd
        Wild-eddying swirl;
Or, thro' the mining outlet bockèd,
          Down headlong hurl:

List'ning the doors an' winnocks rattle,
I thought me on the ourie cattle,
Or silly sheep, wha bide this brattle
        O' winter war,
And thro' the drift, deep-lairing, sprattle
          Beneath a scar.

Ilk happing bird, — wee, helpless thing!
That, in the merry months o' spring,
Delighted me to hear thee sing,
        What comes o' thee?

lift, sky; *wreathes*, drifts; *bocked*, disgorged; *winnocks*, windows; *ourie*, frightened; *bide*, endure; *brattle*, onset; *lairing*, sinking; *sprattle*, struggle; *scar*, rock or cliff; *Ilk*, every; *happing*, hopping.

Whare wilt thou cow'r thy chittering wing,
          An' close thy e'e?

Ev'n you, on murdering errands toil'd,
Lone from your savage homes exil'd,
The blood-stained roost, and sheep-cote spoil'd
          My heart forgets,
While pitiless the tempest wild
          Sore on you beats!

                                        1786

*   *   *

The Holy Fair*

> *A robe of seeming truth and trust*
>   *Hid crafty Observation;*
> *And secret hung, with poison'd crust,*
>   *The dirk of Defamation:*
> *A mask that like the gorget show'd,*
>   *Dye-varying on the pigeon;*
> *And for a mantle large and broad,*
>   *He wrapt him in Religion.*
>   (HYPOCRISY A-LA-MODE)

1

Upon a simmer Sunday morn,
     When Nature's face is fair,
I walked forth to view the corn,
     An' snuff the caller air.
The rising sun, owre Galston muirs,
     Wi' glorious light was glintin;
The hares were hirplin down the furs,
     The lav'rocks they were chantin
               Fu' sweet that day.

simmer, summer; *caller*, fresh; *hirplin*, hopping; *furs*, furrows; *lav'rocks*, larks.

  * Holy Fair is a common phrase in the West of Scotland for a sacramental occasion. (Burns's note.)

II

As lightsomely I glower'd abroad,
   To see a scene sae gay,
Three hizzies, early at the road,
   Cam skelpin up the way.
Twa had manteeles o' dolefu' black,
   But ane wi' lyart lining:
The third, that gaed a wee a-back,
   Was in the fashion shining
               Fu' gay that day.

III

The twa appear'd like sisters twin,
   In feature, form, an' claes;
Their visage wither'd, lang an' thin,
   An' sour as ony slaes:
The third cam up, hap-step-an'-lowp,
   As light as ony lambie,
An' wi' a curchie low did stoop,
   As soon as e'er she saw me,
               Fu' kind that day.

IV

Wi' bonnet aff, quoth I, "Sweet lass,
   I think ye seem to ken me;
I'm sure I've seen that bonie face,
   But yet I canna name ye."
Quo' she, an' laughin as she spak,
   An' taks me by the hauns,
"Ye, for my sake, hae gi'en the feck
   Of a' the ten commauns
               A screed some day.

glowr'd, gazed; *hizzies*, young women; *skelpin*, hurrying; *manteeles*, cloaks; *lyart*, grey; *gaed a wee a-back*, walked a bit behind; *claes*, clothes; *slaes*, sloes; *hap-step-an'-lowp*, hop, skip and jump; *curchie*, curtsey; *hauns*, hands; *feck*, most; *commauns*, commandments; *screed*, rip.

V

"My name is Fun — your cronie dear,
   The nearest friend ye hae;
An' this is Superstition here,
   An' that's Hypocrisy.
I'm gaun to Mauchline Holy Fair,
   To spend an hour in daffin:
Gin ye'll go there, yon runkl'd pair,
   We will get famous laughin
              At them this day."

VI

Quoth I, "With a' my heart, I'll do't;
   I'll get my Sunday's sark on,
An' meet you on the holy spot;
   Faith, we'se hae fine remarkin!"
Then I gaed hame at crowdie-time,
   An' soon I made me ready;
For roads were clad, frae side to side,
   Wi' monie a wearie body,
              In droves that day.

VII

Here, farmers gash, in ridin graith,
   Gaed hoddin by their cotters;
There, swankies young, in braw braid-claith,
   Are springin owre the gutters.
The lasses, skelpin barefit, thrang,
   In silks an' scarlets glitter;
Wi' sweet-milk cheese, in monie a whang,
   An' farls, bak'd wi' butter,
              Fu' crump that day.

gaun, going; *daffin*, merry-making; *Gin*, if; *runkl'd*, wrinkled; *sark*, shirt;
we'se, we'll; *gaed*, went; *crowdie-time*, breakfast time; *gash*, shrewd;
graith, attire; *hoddin*, jogging; *cotters*, cottagers; *swankies*, young bloods;
braw braid-claith, smart broadcloth; *barefit*, barefoot; *thrang*, throng;
whang, large slice; *farls*, oatcakes; *crump*, crisp.

When by the plate we set our nose,
　　Weel heaped up wi' ha'pence,
A greedy glowr Black Bonnet throws,
　　An' we maun draw our tippence.
Then in we go to see the show,
　　On ev'ry side they're gath'rin;
Some carryin dails, some chairs an' stools,
　　An' some are busy bleth'rin
　　　　　　　Right loud that day.

IX

Here stands a shed to fend the show'rs,
　　An' screen our countra Gentry,
There, racer Jess, an' twa-three whores,
　　Are blinkin at the entry.
Here sits a raw o' tittlin Jads,
　　Wi' heaving breast an' bare neck;
An' there, a batch o' wabster lads,
　　Blackguarding frae Kilmarnock
　　　　　　　For fun this day.

X

Here some are thinkin on their sins,
　　An' some upo' their claes;
Ane curses feet that fyl'd his shins,
　　Anither sighs an' prays:
On this hand sits a chosen swatch,
　　Wi' screw'd-up, grace-proud faces;
On that, a set o' chaps, at watch,
　　Thrang winkin on the lasses
　　　　　　　To chairs that day.

glowr, glare; *Black Bonnet*, the Elder; *tippence*, tuppence; *dails*, planks;
twa-three, two or three; *blinkin*, winking; *raw*, row; *tittlin Jads*, tattling
jades; *wabster*, weaver; *claes*, clothes; *fyl'd*, soiled; *swatch*, sample;
Thrang, busy.

XI

O happy is that man an' blest!
  Nae wonder that it pride him!
Wha's ain dear lass, that he likes best,
  Comes clinkin down beside him!
Wi' arm repos'd on the chair-back,
  He sweetly does compose him;
Which, by degrees, slips round her neck,
  An's loof upon her bosom
             Unkend that day.

XII

Now a' the congregation o'er
  Is silent expectation;
For Moodie speels the holy door,
  Wi' tidings o' damnation.
Should Hornie, as in ancient days,
  'Mang sons o' God present him,
The vera sight o' Moodie's face,
  To's ain het hame had sent him
             Wi' fright that day.

XIII

Hear how he clears the points o' faith
  Wi' rattlin an' thumpin!
Now meekly calm, now wild in wrath,
  He's stampin, an' he's jumpin!
His lengthen'd chin, his turn'd-up snout,
  His eldritch squeel an' gestures,
O how they fire the heart devout,
  Like cantharidian plasters,
             On sic a day!

clinkin, dumps herself down; *An's loof*, and his palm; *Unkend*, unnoticed;
speels, climbs; *Hornie*, the Devil; *het*, hot; *eldritch*, unearthly.

XIV

But hark ! the tent has chang'd its voice;
    There's peace an' rest nae langer:
For a' the real judges rise,
    They canna sit for anger.
Smith opens out his cauld harangues,
    On practice and on morals;
An' aff the godly pour in thrangs,
    To gie the jars an' barrels
              A lift that day.

XV

What signifies his barren shine,
    Of moral pow'rs an' reason?
His English style, an' gesture fine,
    Are a' clean out o' season.
Like Socrates or Antonine,
    Or some auld pagan Heathen,
The moral man he does define,
    But ne'er a word o' faith in
              That's right that day.

XVI

In guid time comes an antidote
    Against sic poison'd nostrum;
For Peebles, frae the water-fit,
    Ascends the holy rostrum:
See, up he's got the word o' God,
    An' meek an' mim has view'd it,
While Common-Sense has taen the road,
    An' aff, an' up the Cowgate
              Fast, fast that day.

thrangs, crowds; *shine*, display; *water-fit*, water-foot; *mim*, prim.

Wee Miller niest, the Guard relieves,
 An' Orthodoxy raibles,
Tho' in his heart he weel believes,
 An' thinks it auld wives' fables:
But faith! the birkie wants a Manse,
 So, cannilie he hums them;
Altho' his carnal wit an' sense
 Like hafflins-wise o'ercomes him
    At times that day.

XVIII

Now, butt an' ben the Change-house fills,
 Wi' yill-caup Commentators:
Here's crying out for bakes an' gills,
 An' there the pint-stowp clatters;
While thick an' thrang, an' loud an' lang,
 Wi' Logic, an' wi' Scripture,
They raise a din, that, in the end,
 Is like to breed a rupture
    O' wrath that day.

XIX

Leeze me on Drink! it gies us mair
 Than either School or Colledge:
It kindles Wit, it waukens Lair,
 It pangs us fou o' Knowledge.
Be't whisky gill or penny wheep,
 Or ony stronger potion,
It never fails, on drinkin deep,
 To kittle up our notion,
    By night or day.

niest, next; *raibles*, gabbles; *birkie*, fellow; *Manse*, parish; *cannilie*, artfully; *hums*, humbugs; *hafflins-wise*, nearly half; *butt an' ben*, kitchen and parlour; *Change-house*, tavern; *yill-caup*, ale cup; *bakes*, biscuits; *Leeze me*, my blessings on; *gies mair*, gives more; *waukens*, wakens; *Lair*, learning; *pangs*, crams; *fou*, full; *penny wheep*, small beer; *kittle*, tickle.

XX

The lads an' lasses, blythely bent
   To mind baith saul an' body,
Sir round the table, weel content,
   An' steer about the toddy.
On this ane's dress, an' that ane's leuk,
   They're makin observations;
While some are cozie i' the neuk,
   An' formin assignations
             To meet some day.

XXI

But now the Lord's ain trumpet touts,
   Till a' the hills are rairin,
An' echos back return the shouts;
   Black Russell is na spairin:
His piercing words, like Highlan swords,
   Divide the joints an' marrow;
His talk o' Hell, whare devils dwell,
   Our vera "sauls does harrow"*
             Wi' fright that day!

XXII

A vast, unbottom'd, boundless pit,
   Fill'd fou o' lowin brunstane,
Wha's ragin flame, an' scorchin heat,
   Wad melt the hardest whun-stane!
The half-asleep start up wi' fear,
   An' think they hear it roarin,
When presently it does appear,
   'Twas but some neebor snorin
             Asleep that day.

steer, stir; *leuk*, appearance; *neuk*, corner; *touts*, sounds; *rairin*, roaring;
lowin brunstane, flaming brimstone; *whun-stane*, whin-stone; *neebor*,
neighbour.

* Shakespeare's *Hamlet*. (Burns's note.)

XXIII

'Twad be owre lang a tale to tell,
   How monie stories past,
An' how they crouded to the yill,
   When they were a' dismist:
How drink gaed round, in cogs an' caups,
   Amang the furms an' benches;
An' cheese an' bread, frae women's laps,
   Was dealt about in lunches,
              An' dawds that day.

XXIV

In comes a gaucie, gash Guidwife,
   An' sits down by the fire,
Syne draws her kebbuck an' her knife,
   The lasses they are shyer.
The auld Guidmen, about the grace,
   Frae side to side they bother,
Till some ane by his bonnet lays,
   An' gies them't, like a tether,
              Fu' lang that day.

XXV

Waesucks! for him that gets nae lass,
   Or lasses that hae naething!
Sma' need has he to say a grace,
   Or melvie his braw claithing!
O Wives be mindfu', ance yoursel
   How bonie lads ye wanted,
An' dinna, for a kebbuck-heel,
   Let lasses be affronted
             On sic a day!

yill, ale; *cog*, wooden bowl; *caup*, cup; *furm*, form; *lunches*, large pieces; *dawds*, lumps; *gaucie*, jolly; *gash*, talkative; *Syne*, then; *kebbuck*, cheese; *by*, aside; *tether*, rope; *Waesucks*, alas; *melvie*, soil with meal dust.

XXVI

Now Clinkumbell, wi' rattlin tow,
   Begins to jow an' croon;
Some swagger hame, the best they dow,
   Some wait the afternoon.
At slaps the billies halt a blink,
   Till lasses strip their shoon:
Wi' faith an' hope, an' love an' drink,
   They're a' in famous tune
              For crack that day.

XXVII

How monie hearts this day converts
   O' sinners and o' lasses!
Their hearts o' stane gin night are gane,
   As saft as ony flesh is.
There's some are fou o' love divine;
   There's some are fou o' brandy;
An' monie jobs that day begin,
   May end in Houghmagandie
              Some ither day.

1786

Clinkumbell, the bellringer; *tow*, rope; *jow an' croon*, ring and sound;
dow, can; *slaps*, gaps; *billies*, fellows; *blink*, bit; *strip*, take off; *shoon*,
shoes; *crack*, talk; *gin night*, by nightfall; *gane*, gone; *Houghmagandie*,
fornication.

A Poet's Welcome to His Love-Begotten Daughter

THE FIRST INSTANCE THAT ENTITLED HIM TO THE VENERABLE APPELLATION OF FATHER

Thou's welcome, wean! Mishanter fa' me,
If thoughts o' thee, or yet thy mammie,*
Shall ever daunton me or awe me,
                    My sweet wee lady,
Or if I blush when thou shalt ca' me
                    Tyta or daddie.

Tho' now they ca' me fornicator,
An' tease my name in countra clatter,
The mair they talk, I'm kend the better,
                    E'en let them clash;
An auld wife's tongue's a feckless matter
                    To gie ane fash.

Welcome! my bonie, sweet, wee dochter,
Tho' ye come here a wee unsought for,
And tho' your comin' I hae fought for,
                    Baith kirk and queir;
Yet, by my faith, ye're no unwrought for,
                    That I shall swear!

Sweet fruit o' monie a merry dint,
My funny toil is no a' tint,

---

wean, child; *mishanter fa' me*, Damme!; *countra clatter*, country gossip; *kend*, known; *clash*, talk on; *feckless*, worthless; *gie ane fash*, give a thought to; *dochter*, daughter; *queir*, choir; *dint*, bump; *funny*, full of fun; *tint*, lost.

* Elizabeth Paton, a servant girl at Lochlea. (Ed.)

Tho' thou cam to the warl' asklent,
                    Which fools may scoff at;
In my last plack thy part's be in't
                    The better half o't.

Tho' I should be the waur bestead,
Thou's be as braw and bienly clad,
And thy young years as nicely bred
                    Wi' education,
As onie brat o' wedlock's bed,
                    In a' thy station.

Wee image o' my bonie Betty,
As fatherly I kiss and daut thee,
As dear and near my heart I set thee
                    Wi' as gude will
As a' the priests had seen me get thee
                    That's out o' Hell.

Lord grant that thou may aye inherit
Thy mither's person, grace, an' merit,
An' thy poor, worthless daddy's spirit,
                    Without his failins,
'Twill please me mair to see thee heir it,
                    Than stockit mailens.

For if thou be what I wad hae thee,
An' tak the counsel I shall gie thee,
I'll never rue my trouble wi' thee —
                    The cost nor shame o't,
But be a loving father to thee,
                    And brag the name o't.

1784

warl', world; asklent, waywardly; plack, fourpenny piece Scots; part's, share will be; waur bestead, worse conditioned; braw and bienly, finely and comfortably; onie, any; daut, pet; priests had, priests who might have; That's, who come (i.e. the priests); heir, inherit; stockit mailens, well-stocked farms.

Epistle to J. Lapraik*

AN OLD SCOTTISH BARD

While briers an' woodbines budding green,
And paitricks scraichin loud at e'en,
An' morning poussie whiddin seen,
    Inspire my Muse,
This freedom, in an unknown frien',
    I pray excuse.

On Fasten-een we had a rockin,
To ca' the crack and weave our stockin;
And there was muckle fun and jokin,
    Ye need na doubt;
At length we had a hearty yokin
    At sang about.

There was ae sang, amang the rest,
Aboon them a' it pleas'd me best,
That some kind husband had addrest
    To some sweet wife:
It thirl'd the heart-strings thro' the breast,
    A' to the life.

I've scarce heard ought describ'd sae weel,
What gen'rous, manly bosoms feel;
Thought I, "Can this be Pope or Steele,
    Or Beattie's wark?"
They tald me 'twas an odd kind chiel
    About Muirkirk.

paitricks, partridges; *scraichin*, screaming; *poussie*, hare; *whiddin*, scudding; *Fasten-een*, Shrove Tuesday; *rockin*, party; *ca' the crack*, have a chat; *yokin*, set-to; *Aboon*, above; *thirl'd*, thrilled; *chiel*, fellow.

   * Farmer in Muirkirk. His *Poems on Several Occasions* were published by John Wilson in Kilmarnock (Burns's first publisher) in 1788. (Ed.)

It pat me fidgin-fain to hear't,
An' sae about him there I spier't;
Then a' that ken't him round declar'd,
                              He had ingine,
That nane excell'd it, few cam near't,
                              It was sae fine.

That, set him to a pint of ale,
An' either douce or merry tale,
Or rhymes an' sangs he'd made himsel,
                              Or witty catches,
'Tween Inverness and Tiviotdale,
                              He had few matches.

Then up I gat, an' swoor an aith,
Tho' I should pawn my pleugh an' graith,
Or die a cadger pownie's death,
                              At some dyke-back,
A pint an' gill I'd gie them baith,
                              To hear your crack.

But, first an' foremost, I should tell,
Amaist as soon as I could spell,
I to the crambo-jingle fell,
                              Tho' rude an' rough,
Yet crooning to a body's sel,
                              Does weel eneugh.

I am nae Poet, in a sense,
But just a Rhymer, like, by chance,
An' hae to Learning nae pretence,
                              Yet, what the matter?
Whene'er my Muse does on me glance,
                              I jingle at her.

pat, put; *fidgin-fain*, excited; *spier't*, asked; *ingine*, genius; *douce*, sober;
aith, oath; *pleugh*, plough; *graith*, harness; *cadger pownie*, hawker pony;
dyke, wall; *baith*, both; *crack*, talk; *Amaist*, almost; *crambo-jingle*, rhyming;
crooning, humming; *sel*, self.

Your Critic-folk may cock their nose,
And say, "How can you e'er propose,
You wha ken hardly verse frae prose,
                    To mak a sang?"
But, by your leaves, my learned foes,
                    Ye're maybe wrang.

What's a' your jargon o' your Schools,
Your Latin names for horns an' stools;
If honest Nature made you fools,
                    What sairs your Grammars?
Ye'd better taen up spades and shools,
                    Or knappin-hammers.

A set o' dull, conceited hashes,
Confuse their brains in College-classes!
They gang in stirks, and come out asses,
                    Plain truth to speak;
An' syne they think to climb Parnassus
                    By dint o' Greek!

Gie me ae spark o' Nature's fire,
That's a' the learning I desire;
Then tho' I drudge thro' dub an' mire
                    At pleugh or cart,
My Muse, tho' hamely in attire,
                    May touch the heart.

O for a spunk o' Allan's glee,
Or Ferguson's,* the bauld an' slee,
Or bright Lapraik's, my friend to be,
                    If I can hit it!
That would be lear eneugh for me,
                    If I could get it.

sairs, serves; *taen*, have taken; *shools*, shovels; *knappin*, stone-breaking;
hashes, morons; *stirks*, bullocks; *syne*, then; *dub*, puddle; *hamely*, homely;
spunk, spark; *bauld*, bold; *slee*, subtle; *lear*, learning.

* The poets Allan Ramsay and Robert Fergusson. (Ed.)

Now, Sir, if ye hae friends enow,
Tho' real friends I b'lieve are few,
Yet, if your catalogue be fou,
                    I'se no insist;
But gif ye want ae friend that's true,
                    I'm on your list.

I winna blaw about mysel,
As ill I like my fauts to tell;
But friends an' folks that wish me well,
                    They sometimes roose me;
Tho' I maun own, as monie still
                    As far abuse me.

There's ae wee faut they whyles lay to me,
I like the lasses — Gude forgie me!
For monie a plack they wheedle frae me,
                    At dance or fair;
Maybe some ither thing they gie me
                    They weel can spare.

But Mauchline Race or Mauchline Fair,
I should be proud to meet you there;
We'se gie ae night's discharge to care,
                    If we forgather,
An' hae a swap o' rhymin-ware
                    Wi' ane anither.

The four-gill chap, we'se gar him clatter,
An' kirsen him wi' reekin water;
Syne we'll sit down an' tak our whitter,
                    To chear our heart;
An' faith, we'se be acquainted better
                    Before we part.

fou, full; *I'se*, I'll; *blaw*, brag; *fauts*, faults; *roose*, praise; *maun*, must;
whyles, sometimes; *roose*, flatter; *Gude*, God; *plack*, coin; *chap*, cup;
we'se gar, we'll make; *kirsen*, christen; *reekin*, steaming; *Syne*, then;
whitter, draught.

Awa ye selfish, warly race,
Wha think that havins, sense, an' grace,
Ev'n love an' friendship, should give place
                    To catch-the-plack
I dinna like to see your face,
                    Nor hear your crack.

But ye whom social pleasure charms,
Whose hearts the tide of kindness warms,
Who hold your being on the terms,
                    "Each aid the others,"
Come to my bowl, come to my arms,
                    My friends, my brothers!

But to conclude my lang epistle,
As my auld pen's worn to the grissle;
Twa lines frae you wad gar me fissle,
                    Who am, most fervent,
While I can either sing, or whissle,
                    Your friend and servant.

April 1st, 1785

warly, worldly; *havins*, manners; *catch-the-plack*, making money; *crack*, talk; *fissle*, tingle.

*To William Simpson, Ochiltree**

MAY 1785

I gat your letter, winsome Willie;
Wi' gratefu' heart I thank you brawlie;
Tho' I maun say't, I wad be silly,
                    An' unco vain,
Should I believe, my coaxin billie,
                    Your flatterin strain.

brawlie, heartily; *unco*, very; *billie*, fellow.

* Schoolmaster at Ochiltree. (Ed.)

87

But I'se believe ye kindly meant it,
I sud be laith to think ye hinted
Ironic satire, sidelins sklented
                    On my poor Musie;
Tho' in sic phraisin terms ye've penn'd it,
                    I scarce excuse ye.

My senses wad be in a creel,
Should I but dare a hope to speel,
Wi' Allan, or wi' Gilbertfield,
                    The braes o' fame;
Or Ferguson,* the writer-chiel,
                    A deathless name.

(O Ferguson! thy glorious parts
Ill suited law's dry, musty arts!
My curse upon your whunstane hearts,
                    Ye Enbrugh Gentry!
The tythe o' what ye waste at cartes
                    Wad stow'd his pantry!)

Yet when a tale comes i' my head,
Or lasses gie my heart a screed,
As whiles they're like to be my dead,
                    (O sad disease!)
I kittle up my rustic reed;
                    It gies me ease.

Auld Coila,† now, may fidge fu' fain,
She's gotten Poets o' her ain,

I'se, I'll; *laith*, loth; *sidelins sklented*, sideways squinted; *phraisin*, wheedling; *creel*, whirl; *speel*, climb; *writer-chiel*, lawyer-chap; *whunstane*, whinstone; *cartes*, cards; *Wad stow'd*, would have stuffed; *screed*, rent; *whiles*, sometimes; *dead*, death; *kittle*, tickle; *fidge fu' fain*, tingle with delight; *ain*, own.

* The poets Allan Ramsay, William Hamilton and Robert Fergusson. (Ed.)

† *Coila*, Kyle, Burns's native district of Ayrshire. (Ed.)

Chiels wha their chanters winna hain,
                    But tune their lays,
Till echoes a' resound again
                    Her weel-sung praise.

Nae Poet thought her worth his while,
To set her name in measur'd style;
She lay like some unkend-of isle
                    Beside New Holland,
Or whare wild-meeting oceans boil
                    Besouth Magellan.

Ramsay an' famous Ferguson
Gied Forth an' Tay a lift aboon;
Yarrow an' Tweed, to monie a tune,
                    Owre Scotland rings,
While Irwin, Lugar, Ayr, an' Doon,
                    Naebody sings.

Th' Illissus, Tiber, Thames, an' Seine,
Glide sweet in monie a tunefu' line;
But, Willie, set your fit to mine,
                    An' cock your crest,
We'll gar our streams an' burnies shine
                    Up wi' the best.

We'll sing auld Coila's plains an' fells,
Her moors red-brown wi' heather bells,
Her banks an' braes, her dens an' dells,
                    Whare glorious Wallace
Aft bure the gree, as story tells,
                    Frae Suthron billies.

At Wallace' name, what Scottish blood
But boils up in a spring-tide flood!

chanter, pipe; *hain*, spare; *unkend*, unknown; *aboon*, up; *fit*, foot; *gar*,
make; *bure the gree*, bore off the prize; *billies*, fellows.

Oft have our fearless fathers strode
                    By Wallace' side,
Still pressing onward, red-wat shod,
                    Or glorious dy'd!

O sweet are Coila's haughs an' woods,
When lintwhites chant amang the buds,
And jinkin hares, in amorous whids,
                    Their loves enjoy,
While thro' the braes the cushat croods
                    With wailfu' cry!

Ev'n winter bleak has charms to me
When winds rave thro' the naked tree;
Or frosts on hills of Ochiltree
                    Are hoary gray;
Or blinding drifts wild-furious flee,
                    Dark'ning the day!

O Nature! a' thy shews an' forms
To feeling, pensive hearts hae charms!
Whether the Summer kindly warms,
                    Wi' life an' light,
Or Winter howls, in gusty storms,
                    The lang, dark night!

The Muse, nae Poet ever fand her,
Till by himsel he learn'd to wander,
Adown some trotting burn's meander,
                    An' no think lang;
O sweet, to stray an' pensive ponder
                    A heart-felt sang!

The warly race may drudge an' drive,
Hog-shouther, jundie, stretch an' strive,

red-wat, blood-soaked; haughs, riversides; lintwhites, linnets; jinkin, sporting; whids, gambols; cushat, wood-pigeon; fand, found; warly, worldly; Hog-shouther, push; jundie, jostle.

Let me fair Nature's face descrive,
                         And I, wi' pleasure,
Shall let the busy, grumbling hive
                         Bum owre their treasure.

Fareweel, "My rhyme-composing brither!"
We've been owre lang unkenn'd to ither:
Now let us lay our heads thegither,
                         In love fraternal:
May Envy wallop in a tether,
                         Black fiend, infernal!

While Highlandmen hate tolls an' taxes;
While moorlan herds like guid, fat braxies;
While Terra Firma, on her axis,
                         Diurnal turns,
Count on a friend, in faith an' practice,
                         In Robert Burns.

Bum, buzz; *owre lang unkenn'd*, too long unknown; *ither*, each other;
wallop, kick about; *tether*, rope; *braxies*, dead sheep.

To James Smith*

> *Friendship! mysterious cement of the soul!*
> *Sweetner of Life, and solder of Society!*
> *I owe thee much. —*
>
> BLAIR

Dear Smith, the sleest, paukie thief,
That e'er attempted stealth or rief,
Ye surely hae some warlock-breef
                         Owre human hearts;
For ne'er a bosom yet was prief
                         Against your arts.

sleest, slyest; *paukie*, drily humorous; *rief*, plunder; *warlock-breef*, wizard-
spell; *prief*, proof.

* A boon companion of Burns's who kept a draper's shop in Mauch-
line. (Ed.)

For me, I swear by sun an' moon,
And ev'ry star that blinks aboon,
Ye've cost me twenty pair o' shoon
                    Just gaun to see you;
And ev'ry ither pair that's done,
                    Mair taen I'm wi' you.

That auld, capricious carlin, Nature,
To mak amends for scrimpet stature,
She's turn'd you off, a human creature
                    On her first plan,
And in her freaks, on ev'ry feature,
                    She's wrote, *the Man.*

Just now I've taen the fit o' rhyme,
My barmie noddle's working prime,
My fancy yerkit up sublime
                    Wi' hasty summon:
Hae ye a leisure-moment's time
                    To hear what's comin?

Some rhyme a neebor's name to lash;
Some rhyme (vain thought!) for needfu' cash;
Some rhyme to court the countra clash,
                    An' raise a din;
For me, an aim I never fash;
                    I rhyme for fun.

The star that rules my luckless lot,
Has fated me the russet coat,
An' damn'd my fortune to the groat;
                    But, in requit,
Has blest me wi' a random shot
                    O' countra wit.

aboon, above; *gaun*, going; *taen*, taken; *carlin*, witch; *scrimpet*, stunted;
barmie noddle, fermenting brain; *yerkit*, stimulated; *neebor*, neighbour;
countra clash, country gossip; *fash*, trouble about.

This while my notion's taen a sklent,
To try my fate in guid, black prent;
But still the mair I'm that way bent,
                    Something cries "Hoolie!
I red you, honest man, tak tent!
                    Ye'll shaw your folly.

"There's ither poets, much your betters,
Far seen in Greek, deep men o' letters,
Hae thought they had ensur'd their debtors,
                    A' future ages;
Now moths deform, in shapeless tatters,
                    Their unknown pages".

Then farewel hopes o' laurel-boughs,
To garland my poetic brows!
Henceforth I'll rove where busy ploughs
                    Are whistling thrang,
An' teach the lanely heights an' howes
                    My rustic sang.

I'll wander on, with tentless heed
How never-halting moments speed,
Till fate shall snap the brittle thread;
                    Then, all unknown,
I'll lay me with th'inglorious dead,
                    Forgot and gone!

But why o' Death begin a tale?
Just now we're living, sound an' hale;
Then top and maintop croud the sail,
                    Heave Care o'er-side!
And large, before Enjoyment's gale,
                    Let's tak the tide.

taen, taken; sklent, turn; prent, print; Hoolie!, careful!; red, warn; tent,
heed; shaw, show; thrang, busily; howes, hollows; tentless, careless.

This life, sae far's I understand,
Is a' enchanted fairy-land,
Where Pleasure is the magic wand,
                    That, wielded right,
Maks hours like minutes, hand in hand,
                    Dance by fu' light.

The magic-wand then let us wield;
For, ance that five-an'-forty's speel'd,
See, crazy, weary, joyless Eild,
                    Wi' wrinkl'd face,
Comes hostin, hirplin owre the field,
                    Wi' creepin pace.

When ance life's day draws near the gloamin,
Then fareweel vacant, careless roamin;
An' fareweel chearfu' tankards foamin,
                    An' social noise:
An' fareweel dear, deluding woman,
                    The joy of joys!

O Life! how pleasant in thy morning,
Young Fancy's rays the hills adorning!
Cold-pausing Caution's lesson scorning,
                    We frisk away,
Like school-boys, at th' expected warning,
                    To joy and play.

We wander there, we wander here,
We eye the rose upon the brier,
Unmindful that the thorn is near,
                    Among the leaves;
And tho' the puny wound appear,
                    Short while it grieves.

Some, lucky, find a flow'ry spot,
For which they never toil'd nor swat;

ance, once; *speel'd*, climbed; *Eild*, Age; *hostin*, coughing; *hirplin*, limping; *gloaming*, dusk; *swat*, sweated.

They drink the sweet and eat the fat,
                But care or pain;
And, haply, eye the barren hut
                With high disdain.

With steady aim, some Fortune chase;
Keen hope does ev'ry sinew brace;
Thro' fair, thro' foul, they urge the race,
                And seize the prey:
Then canie, in some cozie place,
                They close the day.

And others, like your humble servan',
Poor wights! nae rules nor roads observin;
To right or left, eternal swervin,
                They zig-zag on;
Till, curst with age, obscure an' starvin,
                They aften groan.

Alas! what bitter toil an' straining —
But truce with peevish, poor complaining!
Is Fortune's fickle *Luna* waning?
                E'en let her gang!
Beneath what light she has remaining,
                Let's sing our sang.

My pen I here fling to the door,
And kneel, "Ye Pow'rs!" and warm implore,
"Tho' I should wander *Terra* o'er,
                In all her climes,
Grant me but this, I ask no more,
                Ay rowth o' rhymes.

"Gie dreeping roasts to countra Lairds,
Till icicles hing frae their beards;

But, without; *canie*, quietly; *rowth*, plenty; *Gie*, give; *dreeping*, dripping;
hing, hang.

Gie fine braw claes to fine Life-guards
                    And Maids of Honor;
And yill an' whisky gie to Cairds,
                    Until they sconner.

"A Title, Dempster* merits it;
A Garter gie to Willie Pitt;
Gie Wealth to some be-ledger'd Cit,
                    In cent. per cent.;
But give me real, sterling Wit,
                    And I'm content.

"While Ye are pleas'd to keep me hale,
I'll sit down o'er my scanty meal,
Be't water-brose, or muslin-kail,
                    Wi' chearfu' face,
As lang's the Muses dinna fail
                    To say the grace."

An anxious e'e I never throws
Behint my lug, or by my nose;
I jouk beneath Misfortune's blows
                    As weel's I may;
Sworn foe to Sorrow, Care, and Prose,
                    I rhyme away.

O ye douce folk, that live by rule,
Grave, tideless-blooded, calm and cool,
Compar'd wi' you — O fool! fool! fool!
                    How much unlike!
Your hearts are just a standing pool,
                    Your lives, a dyke!

claes, clothes; *yill*, ale; *cairds*, tinkers; *sconner*, are disgusted; *water-brose*,
meal and water; *muslin-kail*, thin broth; *lug*, ear; *jouk*, duck; *douce*, sober;
dyke, wall.

* A patriotic Scots M.P., "Honest George". (Ed.)

Nae hair-brain'd, sentimental traces,
In your unletter'd, nameless faces!
In *arioso* trills and graces
                    Ye never stray,
But *gravissimo*, solemn basses
                    Ye hum away.

Ye are sae grave, nae doubt ye're wise;
Nae ferly tho' ye do despise
The hairum-scairum, ram-stam boys,
                    The rattling squad:
I see you upward cast your eyes —
                    — Ye ken the road —

Whilst I — but I shall haud me there —
Wi' you I'll scarce gang ony where —
Then, Jamie, I shall say nae mair,
                    But quat my sang.
Content with You to mak a pair,
                    Whare'er I gang.

                                        1786

ferly, wonder; *ram-stam*, headlong; *rattling*, roistering; *haud*, hold; *quat*,
quit.

To a Louse

ON SEEING ONE ON A LADY'S BONNET AT CHURCH

Ha! whare ye gaun, ye crowlin ferlie!
Your impudence protects you sairlie:
I canna say but ye strunt rarely,
                    Owre gauze and lace;
Tho' faith, I fear, ye dine but sparely
                    On sic a place.

gaun, going; *crowlin*, crawling; *ferlie*, marvel; *sairlie*, well; *strunt*, strut.

B.P.S.

Ye ugly, creepin, blastit wonner,
Detested, shunn'd, by saunt an' sinner,
How daur ye set your fit upon her,
        Sae fine a Lady!
Gae somewhere else and seek your dinner,
        On some poor body.

Swith, in some beggar's haffet squattle;
There ye may creep, and sprawl, and sprattle
Wi' ither kindred, jumping cattle,
        In shoals and nations;
Whare horn nor bane ne'er daur unsettle
        Your thick plantations.

Now haud you there, ye're out o' sight,
Below the fatt'rels, snug and tight;
Na faith ye yet! ye'll no be right
        Till ye've got on it,
The vera tapmost, tow'ring height
        O' Miss's bonnet.

My sooth! right bauld ye set your nose out,
As plump an' gray as onie grozet:
O for some rank, mercurial rozet,
        Or fell, red smeddum,
I'd gie ye sic a hearty dose o't
        Wad dress your droddum!

I wad na been surpris'd to spy
You on an auld wife's flainen toy;

blastit wonner, confounded wonder; *saunt*, saint; *daur*, dare; *fit*, foot;
Swith, Begone!; *baffet*, short hair on temple; *squattle*, squat; *sprattle*,
scramble; *born nor bane* (bone), i.e. combs; *haud*, keep; *fatt'rels*, fal-de-rals;
tapmost, topmost; *bauld*, boldly; *grozet*, gooseberry; *rozet*, rosin; *fell*,
deadly; *smeddum*, powder; *sic*, such; *droddum*, breech; *wad na*, would not
have; *flainen toy*, flannel cap.

Or aiblins some bit duddie boy,
                    On's wyliecoat;
But Miss's fine Lunardi! fye!
                    How daur ye do't?

O Jenny, dinna toss your head,
An' set your beauties a' abread!
Ye little ken what cursed speed
                    The blastie's makin!
Thae winks and finger-ends, I dread,
                    Are notice takin!

O wad some Pow'r the giftie gie us
To see oursels as others see us!
It wad frae monie a blunder free us
                    An' foolish notion:
What airs in dress an' gait wad lea'e us,
                    An' ev'n Devotion!

1786

aiblins, maybe; *bit duddie*, small ragged; *wyliecoat*, vest; *Lunardi*, balloon bonnet; *abread*, abroad; *blastie*, wretch; *Thae*, those; *lea'e*, leave.

Such a Parcel of Rogues in a Nation

Fareweel to a' our Scottish fame,
    Fareweel our ancient glory;
Fareweel ev'n to the Scottish name,
    Sae fam'd in martial story!
Now Sark rins over Solway sands,
    An' Tweed rins to the ocean,
To mark where England's province stands —
    Such a parcel of rogues in a nation!

rins, runs.

What force or guile could not subdue,
    Thro' many warlike ages,
Is wrought now by a coward few,
    For hireling traitor's wages.
The English steel we could disdain,
    Secure in valour's station;
But English gold has been our bane —
    Such a parcel of rogues in a nation!

O would, or I had seen the day
    That Treason thus could sell us,
My auld grey head had lien in clay
    Wi' Bruce and loyal Wallace!
But pith and power, till my last hour
    I'll mak this declaration
We're bought and sold for English gold —
    Such a parcel of rogues in a nation!

or, before.

Address of Beelzebub

To the Rt. Hon. the Earl of Breadalbane, President of The Rt. Honorable The Highland Society, which met on the 23rd of May last, at The Shakespeare, Covent Garden, to concert ways and means to frustrate the designs of Five Hundred Highlanders who, as The Society were informed by Mr. Mackenzie of Applecross, were so audacious as to attempt an escape from their lawful lords and masters whose property they were, by emigrating from the lands of Mr. M'Donald of Glengary to the wilds of Canada, in search of that fantastic thing — Liberty!

Long life, my lord, an' health be yours,
Unskaithed by hunger'd Highland boors;
Lord grant nae duddie, desperate beggar,
Wi' dirk, claymore, and rusty trigger,
May twin auld Scotland o' a life
She likes — as lambkins like a knife.

duddie, ragged; *twin*, bereave.

100

Faith you and Applecross were right
To keep the Highland hounds in sight:
I doubt na! they wad bid nae better,
Than let them ance out owre the water,
Then up amang thae lakes and seas,
They'll mak what rules and laws they please:
Some daring Hancock, or a Franklin,
May set their Highland bluid a-ranklin;
Some Washington again may head them,
Or some Montgomery, fearless, lead them;
Till (God knows what may be effected
When by such heads and hearts directed)
Poor dunghill sons of dirt and mire
May to Patrician rights aspire!
Nae sage North now, nor sager Sackville,
To watch and premier o'er the pack vile, —
An' whare will ye get Howes and Clintons
To bring them to a right repentence —
To cowe the rebel generation,
An' save the honour o' the nation?
They, an' be damn'd! what right hae they
To meat, or sleep, or light o' day?
Far less to riches, pow'r, or freedom,
But what your lordship likes to gie them?

But hear, my lord! Glengary hear!
Your hand's owre light on them, I fear;
Your factors, grieves, trustees, and bailies,
I canna say but they do gaylies;
They lay aside a' tender mercies,
An' tirl the hullions to the birses;
Yet while they're only poind and herriet,
They'll keep their stubborn Highland spirit:
But smash them! crush them a' to spails,
An' rot the dyvors i' the jails!

bid, wish; *ance*, once; *owre*, over; *thae*, those; *owre*, too; *grieves*, managers;
gaylies, splendidly; *tirl*, force; *hullions*, good-for-nothings; *birses*, scrubland;
poind, imprisoned; *herriet*, persecuted; *spails*, splinters; *dyvors*, broken men.

The young dogs, swinge them to the labour;
Let wark an' hunger mak them sober!
The hizzies, if they're aughtlins fawsont,
Let them in Drury-Lane be lesson'd!
An' if the wives an' dirty brats
Come thiggin at your doors an' yetts,
Flaffin wi' duds, an' grey wi' beas',
Frightin awa your deuks an' geese;
Get out a horsewhip or a jowler,
The langest thong, the fiercest growler,
An' gar the tatter'd gypsies pack
Wi' a' their bastards on their back!

Go on, my Lord! I lang to meet you,
And in my house at hame to greet you;
Wi' common lords ye shanna mingle,
The benmost neuk beside the ingle,
At my right han' assigned your seat,
'Tween Herod's hip an' Polycrate:
Or (if you on your station tarrow),
Between Almagro and Pizarro,
A seat, I'm sure ye're weel deservin't;
An' till ye come — your humble servant,

                                        BEELZEBUB

*Hell, June 1st, Anno Mundi 5790**

swinge, whip; wark, work; hizzies, girls; aughtlins fawsont, at all attractive; thiggin, begging; yetts, gates; Flaffin, flapping; duds, rags; beas', vermin; jowler, foxhound; gar, compel; benmost neuk, inmost corner; tarrow, complain.

* Archbishop Ussher of Armagh calculated that God created the world in 4004 B.C. (Ed.)

Written by Somebody on the Window

OF AN INN AT STIRLING, ON SEEING
THE ROYAL PALACE IN RUINS

Here Stuarts once in glory reigned,
And laws for Scotland's weal ordained;
But now unroof'd their palace stands,
Their sceptre fallen to other hands;
Fallen indeed, and to the earth
Whence grovelling reptiles take their birth.
The injured Stuart line is gone,
A race outlandish fills their throne;
An idiot race, to honour lost;
Who know them best despise them most.

1787

Scotch Drink

Gie him strong drink until he wink,
  That's sinking in despair;
An' liquor guid to fire his bluid,
  That's prest wi' grief an' care:
There let him bowse an' deep carouse,
  Wi' bumpers flowing o'er,
Till he forgets his loves or debts,
  An' minds his briefs no more.
  SOLOMON'S *Proverbs*, xxxi, 6, 7

Let other poets raise a fracas
'Bout vines, an' wines, an' druken Bacchus,
An' crabbed names an' stories wrack us,
              An' grate our lug,
I sing the juice Scotch bear can mak us,
              In glass or jug.

lug, ear; *bear,* barley.
103

O thou, my Muse! guid, auld Scotch Drink!
Whether thro' wimplin worms thou jink,
Or, richly brown, ream owre the brink,
                In glorious faem,
Inspire me, till I lisp an' wink,
                To sing thy name!

Let husky wheat the haughs adorn,
And aits set up their awnie horn,
An' pease an' beans, at een or morn,
                Perfume the plain,
Leeze me on thee, John Barleycorn,
                Thou king o' grain!

On thee aft Scotland chows her cood,
In souple scones, the wale o' food!
Or tumbling in the boiling flood
                Wi' kail an' beef;
But when thou pours thy strong heart's blood,
                There thou shines chief.

Food fills the wame, an' keeps us livin;
Tho' life's a gift no worth receivin;
When heavy-dragg'd wi' pine an' grievin;
                But oil'd by thee,
The wheels o' life gae down-hill, scrievin,
                Wi' rattlin glee.

Thou clears the head o' doited Lear;
Thou chears the heart o' drooping Care;

wimplin, winding; *worm*, a serpentine distilling tube; *jink*, dodge; *ream*, froth; *haugh*, flat ground by stream; *Aits*, oats; *awnie*, bearded; *Leeze me on*, Bless thee (an expression of great pleasure or affection); *chows*, chews; *cood*, cud; *souple*, limp, soft; *wale*, choice, pick; *kail*, broth; *wame*, belly; *pine*, misery; *gae*, go; *scrievin*, rolling; *rattlin*, rollicking; *doited*, stupefied; *Lear*, learning.

Thou strings the nerves o' Labor-fair,
                    At's weary toil;
Thou ev'n brightens dark Despair,
                    Wi' gloomy smile.

Aft, clad in massy, siller weed,
Wi' Gentles thou erects thy head;
Yet humbly kind, in time o' need,
                    The poor man's wine;
His wee drap pirratch, or his bread,
                    Thou kitchens fine.

Thou art the life o' public haunts;
But thee, what were our fairs and rants?
Ev'n godly meetings o' the saunts,
                    By thee inspir'd,
When gaping they besiege the tents,
                    Are doubly fir'd.

That merry night we get the corn in,
O sweetly, then, thou reams the horn in!
Or reekan on a New-year-mornin
                    In cog or bicker,
An' just a wee drap sp'ritual burn in,
                    An' gusty sucker!

When Vulcan gies his bellys breath,
An' Ploughmen gather wi' their graith,
O rare! to see thee fizz and freath
                    I' the lugget caup!
Then Burnewin comes on like Death
                    At ev'ry chap.

weed, dress; _pirratch_, porridge; _kitchen_, season, flavour; _But_, without;
rants, revels, merry-makings; _saunts_, saints; _gaping_, dying for a drink;
reams, foams; _reekan_, steaming (i.e. hot toddy); _cog_, wooden cup or bowl;
bicker, wooden beaker or cup; _burn_, brew; _gusty_, tasty; _sucker_, sugar;
bellys, bellows; _graith_, gear; _freath_, froth; _lugget caup_, two-eared cup,
quaich; _Burnewin_, Burn-the-wind (i.e. the blacksmith); _chap_, stroke.

Nae mercy, then, for airn or steel;
The brawnie, banie, ploughman-chiel
Brings hard owrehip, wi' sturdy wheel,
                    The strong forehammer,
Till block and studdie ring an' reel
                    Wi dinsome clamour.

When skirlin weanies see the light,
Thou maks the gossips clatter bright,
How fumbling coofs their dearies slight,
                    Wae worth them for't!
While healths gae round to him wha, tight,
                    Gies famous sport.

When neebors anger at a plea,
An' just as wud as wud can be,
How easy can the barley-brie
                    Cement the quarrel!
It's aye the cheapest lawyer's fee
                    To taste the barrel.

Alake! that e'er my Muse has reason,
To wyte her countrymen wi' treason!
But monie daily weet their weason
                    Wi liquors nice,
An' hardly, in a winter season,
                    E'er spier her price.

Wae worth that Brandy, burnan trash!
Fell source o' monie a pain an' brash!

airn, iron; *banie*, bony; *studdie*, anvil; *skirlin*, screaming; *weanies*, infants; *gossips*, godparents or old friends; *clatter*, gossip; *coofs*, fools; *flight*, put to flight; *Wae worth them*, bad luck to them; *tight*, manly; *neebors*, neighbours; *wud*, angry; *barley-brie* (brew), whisky; *wyte*, blame; *weet*, wet; *weason*, throat; *spier*, ask; *Wae worth*, Alas!; *brash*, sudden illness, an "attack".

Twins monie a poor, doylt, druken hash
                    O' half his days;
An' sends, beside, auld Scotland's cash
                    To her warst faes.

Ye Scots wha wish auld Scotland well,
Ye chief, to you my tale I tell,
Poor, plackless devils like mysel,
                    It sets you ill,
Wi' bitter, dearthfu' wines to mell,
                    Or foreign gill.

May gravels round his blather wrench,
An' gouts torment him, inch by inch,
Wha twists his gruntle wi' a glunch
                    O' sour disdain,
Out owre a glass o' Whisky-punch
                    Wi' honest men!

O Whisky! soul o' ploys an' pranks!
Accept a Bardie's gratefu' thanks!
When wanting thee, what tuneless cranks
                    Are my poor verses!
Thou comes — they rattle i' their ranks
                    At ither's arses!

Thee, Ferintosh! O sadly lost!
Scotland lament frae coast to coast!

Twins, separates; doylt, crazed; druken, drunken; hash, mess of a man;
warst faes, worst foes; chief, chiefly; plackless, penniless; dearthfu', expen-
sive; mell, mix; blather, bladder; gruntle, snout; glunch, frown; wanting,
without; cranks, creakings; rattle, dash, run ahead.

Now colic-grips, an' barkin hoast,
                    May kill us a';
For loyal Forbes' charter'd boast
                    Is taen awa !*

Thae curst horse-leeches o' th'Excise,
Wha mak the whisky stells their prize !
Haud up thy han', Deil ! ance, twice, thrice !
                    There, sieze the blinkers !
An' bake them up in brunstane pies
                    For poor d——n'd drinkers.

Fortune, if thou'll but gie me still
Hale breeks, a scone, an' whisky gill,
An' rowth o' rhyme to rave at will,
                    Tak a' the rest,
An' deal't about as thy blind skill
                    Directs thee best.

                                                    1785

boast, cough; *taen*, taken; *stells*, stills; *Haud*, hold; *han'*, hand; *brunstane*, brimstone; *gie*, give; *Hale*, whole; *rowth*, abundance.

* The Ferintosh Distillery in Cromarty was owned by Duncan Forbes of Culloden (1644–1704). He was exempted from payment of excise duty in perpetuity for his services during the "Glorious Revolution" of 1690 which dethroned the Catholic James VII and II and enthroned the Protestant William of Orange and Mary Stuart. This exemption was abolished in 1785. (Ed.)

The Deil's awa wi' th' Exciseman

The deil cam fiddlin thro' the town,
  And danc'd awa wi' th' Exciseman;
And ilka wife cries, auld Mahoun,
  I wish you luck o' the prize, man.

The deil's awa, the deil's awa
  The deil's awa wi' th' Exciseman,
He's danc'd awa, he's danc'd awa
  He's danc'd awa wi' th' Exciseman.

We'll mak our maut and we'll brew our drink,
  We'll laugh, sing, and rejoice, man;
And mony braw thanks to the meikle black deil,
  That danc'd awa wi' th' Exciseman.

There's threesome reels, there's foursome reels,
  There's hornpipes and strathspeys, man,
But the ae best dance e'er cam to the Land
  Was, the deil's awa wi' th' Exciseman.

1792

ilka, every; *Mahoun*, devil (Mahomed); *maut*, malt; *braw*, hearty; *meikle*, big.

To a Haggis

Fair fa' your honest, sonsie face,
Great Chieftain o' the Puddin-race!
Aboon them a' ye tak your place,
          Painch, tripe, or thairm:
Weel are ye wordy of a grace
          As lang's my arm.

Fair fa', blessings on; *sonsie*, jolly; *Aboon*, above; *Painch*, paunch; *thairm*, small guts; *wordy*, worthy.

The groaning trencher there ye fill,
Your hurdies like a distant hill,
Your pin wad help to mend a mill
                    In time o' need,
While thro' your pores the dews distil
                    Like amber bead.

His knife see Rustic-labour dight,
An' cut you up wi' ready slight,
Trenching your gushing entrails bright
                    Like onie ditch;
And then, O what a glorious sight,
                    Warm-reekin, rich!

Then, horn for horn they stretch an' strive,
Deil tak the hindmost, on they drive,
Till a' their weel-swall'd kytes belyve
                    Are bent like drums;
Then auld Guidman, maist like to rive,
                    Bethankit hums.

Is there that owre his French *ragout*,
Or *olio* that wad staw a sow,
Or *fricassee* wad mak her spew
                    Wi' perfect sconner
Looks down wi' sneering, scornfu' view
                    On sic a dinner?

Poor devil! see him owre his trash,
As feckless as a wither'd rash,
His spindle shank a guid whip-lash,
                    His nieve a nit;
Thro' bluidy flood or field to dash,
                    O how unfit!

hurdies, buttocks; *dight*, wipe; *slight*, skill; *-reekin*, -smoking; *horn*, horn-spoon; *weel-swall'd kytes*, well-swelled stomachs; *belyve*, by-and-bye; *maist*, almost; *rive*, burst; *staw*, surfeit; *sconner*, disgust; *feckless*, feeble; *rash*, rush; *nieve*, fist; *nit*, nut.

But mark the Rustic, haggis-fed,
The trembling earth resounds his tread,
Clap in his walie nieve a blade,
          He'll mak it whissle;
An' legs, an' arms, an' heads will sned,
          Like taps o' thrissle.

Ye Pow'rs wha mak mankind your care,
And dish them out their bill o' fare,
Auld Scotland wants nae skinking ware,
          That jaups in luggies;
But, if ye wish her gratefu' prayer,
          Gie her a Haggis!

1786

walie nieve, ample fist; *sned*, lop; *taps o' thrissle*, tops of thistle; *skinking*, watery; *jaups*, splashes; *luggies*, wooden bowls.

On the Late Captain Grose's Peregrinations thro' Scotland

COLLECTING THE ANTIQUITIES OF THAT KINGDOM

Hear, Land o' Cakes, and brither Scots,
Frae Maidenkirk to Johny Groats! —
If there's a hole in a' your coats,
          I rede you tent it:
A chield's amang you, taking notes,
          And, faith, he'll prent it.

rede, advise; *tent*, look to; *chield*, fellow; *prent*, print.

If in your bounds ye chance to light
Upon a fine, fat, fodgel wight,
O' stature short, but genius bright,
                    That's he, mark weel —
And wow! he has an unco slight
                    O' cauk and keel.

By some auld, houlet-haunted biggin,*
Or kirk deserted by its riggin,
It's ten to ane ye'll find him snug in
                    Some eldritch part,
Wi' deils, they say, Lord safe's! colleaguin
                    At some black art.

Ilk ghaist that haunts auld ha' or chamer,
Ye gipsy-gang that deal in glamor,
And you, deep-read in hell's black grammar,
                    Warlocks and witches;
Ye'll quake at his conjuring hammer,
                    Ye midnight bitches.

It's tauld he was a sodger bred,
And ane wad rather fa'n than fled;
But now he's quat the spurtle-blade,
                    And dog-skin wallet,
And taen the — Antiquarian trade,
                    I think they call it.

He has a fouth o' auld nick-nackets:
Rusty airn caps and jingling jackets,

---

fodgel, dumpy; slight, skill; cauk and keel, chalk and pencil; houlet, owl; biggin, dwelling; riggin, roof; safe's, save us; colleaguin, conspiring; Ilk, each; ghaist, ghost; ha', hall; chamer, chamber; glamor, magic; wad, would have; fa'n, fallen; quat, quitted; spurtle-, sword-; taen, taken; fouth, abundance; airn, iron.

* Vide his Antiquities of Scotland. (Burns's note, referring to "Tam o' Shanter" which he wrote for Grose's book. Ed.)

Wad haud the Lothians three in tackets,
                    A towmont gude;
And parritch-pats, and auld saut-backets,
                    Before the Flood.

Of Eve's first fire he has a cinder;
Auld Tubalcain's fire-shool and fender;
That which distinguishèd the gender
                    O' Balaam's ass;
A broom-stick o' the witch of Endor,
                    Weel shod wi' brass.

Forbye, he'll shape you aff fu' gleg
The cut of Adam's philibeg;
The knife that nicket Abel's craig
                    He'll prove you fully,
It was a faulding jocteleg,
                    Or lang-kail gullie. —

But wad ye see him in his glee,
For meikle glee and fun has he,
Then set him down, and twa or three
                    Gude fellows wi' him;
And port, O port! shine thou a wee,
                    And THEN ye'll see him!

Now, by the Pow'rs o' Verse and Prose!
Thou art a dainty chield, O Grose! —
Whae'er o' thee shall ill suppose,
                    They sair misca' thee;
I'd take the rascal by the nose,
                    Wad say, Shame fa' thee.

                                        1785

Wad haud, would keep; *tackets*, shoenails; *towmont*, twelvemonth;
parritch-pats, porridge-pots; *saut-backets*, salt-boxes; *shool*, shovel; *Forbye*,
besides; *gleg*, smartly; *philibeg*, kilt; *nicket*, cut; *craig*, throat; *faulding
jocteleg*, folding claspknife; *lang-kail gullie*, cabbage knife; *meikle*, much;
dainty chield, splendid chap; *sair misca'*, much malign; *fa'*, befall.

Written in a Wrapper Inclosing a Letter to Captn Grose

TO BE LEFT WITH MR CARDONNEL, ANTIQUARIAN

Ken ye ought o' Captain Grose?
Igo & ago,
If he's amang his friends or foes?
Iram coram dago.

Is he South, or is he North?
Igo & ago,
Or drowned in the river Forth?
Iram coram dago.

Is he slain by Highland bodies?
Igo & ago,
And eaten like a weather-haggis?
Iram coram dago.

Is he to Abram's bosom gane?
Igo & ago,
Or haudin Sarah by the wame?
Iram coram dago.

Whare'er he be, the Lord be near him!
Igo & ago,
As for the deil, he daur na steer him,
Iram coram dago.

But please transmit th' inclosed letter,
Igo & ago,
Which will oblidge your humble debtor,
Iram coram dago.

bodies, blokes; *weather-haggis*, haggis boiled in a sheep's stomach; *haudin*, holding; *wame*, belly; *daur na*, dare not; *steer*, meddle with.

So may ye hae auld stanes in store,
        Igo & ago,
The very stanes that Adam bore;
        Iram coram dago.

So may ye get in glad possession,
        Igo & ago,
The coins o' Satan's Coronation!
        Iram coram dago.

1790

hae auld stanes, have old stones.

Mary Morison*

O Mary, at thy window be,
  It is the wish'd, the trysted hour;
Those smiles and glances let me see,
  That make the miser's treasure poor:
  How blythly wad I bide the stoure,
A weary slave frae sun to sun;
  Could I the rich reward secure,
The lovely Mary Morison.

Yestreen when to the trembling string,
  The dance gaed thro' the lighted ha',
To thee my fancy took its wing,
  I sat, but neither heard or saw:
  Tho' this was fair, and that was braw,
And yon the toast of a' the town,
  I sigh'd, and said amang them a',
"Ye are na Mary Morison."

trysted, appointed; *bide*, endure; *stoure*, turmoil; *Yestreen*, last night; *ha'*, hall; *braw*, fine; *yon*, the other.

  * Generally supposed to have been Alison Begbie whom the poet courted in his 23rd year but who refused his offer of marriage. (Ed.)

O Mary, canst thou wreck his peace,
  Wha for thy sake wad gladly die!
Or canst thou break that heart of his,
  Whase only faut is loving thee.
If love for love thou wilt na gie,
At least be pity to me shown;
  A thought ungentle canna be
The thought o' Mary Morison.

1780

faut, fault; *gie*, give; *canna*, cannot.

Corn Riggs

Tune: "Corn rigs are bonie"

It was upon a Lammas night,
  When corn rigs are bonie,
Beneath the moon's unclouded light,
  I held awa to Annie:
The time flew by, wi' tentless heed,
  Till, 'tween the late and early;
Wi' sma' persuasion she agreed,
  To see me thro' the barley.

      Corn rigs, an' barley rigs,
        An' corn rigs are bonie:
      I'll ne'er forget that happy night
        Amang the rigs wi' Annie.

Lammas, autumn; *rigs*, ridges; *tentless*, careless.

The sky was blue, the wind was still,
   The moon was shining clearly;
I set her down, wi' right good will,
   Amang the rigs o' barley:
I ken't her heart was a' my ain;
   I lov'd her most sincerely;
I kiss'd her owre and owre again,
   Amang the rigs o' barley.

I lock'd her in my fond embrace;
   Her heart was beating rarely:
My blessings on that happy place,
   Amang the rigs o' barley!
But by the moon and stars so bright,
   That shone that hour so clearly!
She ay shall bless that happy night,
   Amang the rigs o' barley.

I hae been blythe wi' comrades dear;
   I hae been merry drinking;
I hae been joyfu' gath'rin gear;
   I hae been happy thinking:
But a' the pleasures e'er I saw,
   Tho' three times doubl'd fairly,
That happy night was worth them a',
   Amang the rigs o' barley.

1783

ain, own; *gath'rin gear*, making money.

Green Grow the Rashes, O

     Green grow the rashes, O;
     Green grow the rashes, O;
     The sweetest hours that e'er I spent,
     Are spent amang the lasses, O.

117

There's nought but care on ev'ry han',
  In every hour that passes, O:
What signifies the life o' man,
  An' 'twere na for the lasses, O.

The warly race may riches chase,
  An' riches still may fly them, O;
An' tho' at last they catch them fast,
  Their hearts can ne'er enjoy them, O.

But gie me a cannie hour at e'en,
  My arms about my Dearie, O;
An' warly cares, an' warly men,
  May a' gae tapsalteerie, O!

For you sae douse, ye sneer at this,
  Ye're nought but senseless asses, O:
The wisest Man the warl' e'er saw,
  He dearly lov'd the lasses, O.

Auld Nature swears, the lovely Dears
  Her noblest work she classes, O:
Her prentice han' she try'd on man,
  An' then she made the lasses, O.

1784

warly, worldly; *cannie*, quiet; *tapsalteerie*, topsy-turvy; *douse*, sober.

Wha is That at My Bower-Door?

"Wha is that at my bower-door?"
  'O wha is it but Findlay!'
"Then gae your gate, ye'se nae be here:"
  'Indeed maun I,' quo' Findlay.

gae your gate, go your way; *maun*, must.

"What mak' ye, sae like a thief?'
  'O come and see,' quo' Findlay.
"Before the morn ye'll work mischief:"
  'Indeed will I,' quo' Findlay.

"Gif I rise and let you in" —
  'Let me in,' quo' Findlay;
"Ye'll keep me waukin wi' your din:"
  'Indeed will I,' quo' Findlay.
"In my bower if ye should stay" —
  'Let me stay,' quo' Findlay;
"I fear ye'll bide till break o' day:"
  'Indeed will I,' quo' Findlay.

"Here this night if ye remain" —
  'I'll remain,' quo' Findlay;
"I dread ye'll learn the gate again:"
  'Indeed will I,' quo' Findlay.
"What may pass within this bower" —
  'Let it pass,' quo' Findlay;
"Ye maun conceal till your last hour:"
  'Indeed will I,' quo' Findlay.

1784

mak' ye, are you up to; *waukin*, waking; *gate*, way.

Scroggam, My Dearie

There was a wife wonn'd in Cockpen,
        Scroggam;
She brew'd gude ale for gentlemen;
  Sing auld Cowl lay ye down by me,
    Scroggam, my dearie, ruffum.

wonn'd, lived; *Cowl*, parish priest of Cockpen, Midlothian (Ed.)

119

The gudewife's dochter fell in a fever,
            Scroggam;
The priest o' the parish fell in anither;
    Sing auld Cowl lay ye down by me,
        Scroggam, my dearie, ruffum.

They laid the twa i' the bed thegither,
            Scroggam;
That the heat o' the tane might cool the tither;
    Sing auld Cowl, lay ye down by me,
        Scroggam, my dearie, ruffum.

dochter, daughter; *tane . . . tither*, one . . . other.

Guid Ale Keeps the Heart Aboon

O gude ale comes and gude ale goes;
Gude ale gars me sell my hose,
Sell my hose, and pawn my shoon --
Gude ale keeps my heart aboon!

I had sax owsen in a pleugh,
And they drew a' weel eneugh:
I sell'd them a' just ane by ane —
Gude ale keeps the heart aboon!

Gude ale hauds me bare and busy,
Gars me moop wi' the servant hizzie,
Stand i' the stool when I hae done —
Gude ale keeps the heart aboon!

Aboon, high; *owsen*, oxen; *ane*, one; *gars*, forces me to; *hauds*, keeps; *moop*, meddle; *hizzie*, hussy; *stool*, repentance or cutty stool.

Up in the Morning Early

Cauld blaws the wind frae east to west,
    The drift is driving sairly;
Sae loud and shill's I hear the blast,
    I'm sure it's winter fairly.

          Up in the morning's no for me,
            Up in the morning early;
          When a' the hills are cover'd wi' snaw,
            I'm sure it is winter fairly.

The birds sit chittering in the thorn,
    A' day they fare but sparely;
And lang's the night frae e'en to morn,
    I'm sure it's winter fairly.

1788

sairly, hard; *shill*, shrill; *snaw*, snow; *chittering*, shivering.

My Love She's but a Lassie yet

          My love she's but a lassie yet,
          My love she's but a lassie yet,
          We'll let her stand a year or twa,
          She'll no be half sae saucy yet.

I rue the day I sought her O,
I rue the day I sought her O,
Wha gets her needs na say he's woo'd,
But he may say he's bought her O.

Come draw a drap o' the best o't yet,
Come draw a drap o' the best o't yet:
Gae seek for pleasure whare ye will,
But here I never misst it yet.

121

We're a' dry wi' drinking o't,
We're a' dry wi' drinking o't:
The minister kisst the fidler's wife,
He could na preach for thinkin o't.

1788

I'm o'er Young to Marry yet

I am my mammy's ae bairn,
   Wi' unco folk I weary, Sir,
And lying in a man's bed,
   I'm fley'd it make me irie, Sir.

        I'm o'er young, I'm o'er young,
        I'm o'er young to marry yet;
        I'm o'er young, 'twad be a sin
        To tak me frae my mammy yet.

Hallowmass is come and gane,
   The nights are lang in winter, Sir;
And you and I in ae bed,
   In trowth, I dare na venture, Sir.

Fu' loud and shill the frosty wind
   Blaws thro' the leafless timmer, Sir;
But if ye come this gate again,
   I'll aulder be gin simmer, Sir.

1788

o'er, too; *ae bairn*, only child; *unco*, strange; *fley'd* . . ., afraid I'd be
scared; *shill*, shrill; *timmer*, woods; *gate*, way; *aulder be gin simmer*, older be
by summer.

Ay Waukin, O

Simmer's a pleasant time,
  Flowers of ev'ry colour;
The water rins o'er the heugh,
  And I long for my true lover!

              Ay waukin, O,
                Waukin still and weary:
              Sleep I can get nane,
                For thinking on my dearie.

When I sleep I dream,
  When I wauk I'm irie;
Sleep I can get nane
  For thinking on my dearie.

Lanely night comes on,
  A' the lave are sleepin:
I think on my bony lad
  And I bleer my een wi' greetin.

Waukin, waking; *Simmer*, summer; *rins*, runs; *heugh*, crag; *nane*, none;
irie, sad; *lave*, rest; *greetin*, weeping.

John Anderson, My Jo

John Anderson my jo, John,
  When we were first acquent;
Your locks were like the raven,
  Your bony brow was brent;
But now your brow is beld, John,
  Your locks are like the snaw;
But blessings on your frosty pow,
  John Anderson my jo.

Jo, dear; *acquent*, acquainted; *brent*, smooth; *beld*, bald; *pow*, head.

John Anderson my jo, John,
  We clamb the hill thegither;
And mony a canty day John,
  We've had wi' ane anither;
Now we maun totter down, John,
  And hand in hand we'll go;
And sleep thegither at the foot,
  John Anderson my jo.

1788

clamb, climbed; *thegither*, together; *canty*, cheerful; *ane anither*, one another; *maun*, have to.

What can a Young Lassie Do wi' an Auld Man?

What can a young lassie, what shall a young lassie,
  What can a young lassie do wi' an auld man?
Bad luck on the penny that tempted my minnie
  To sell her puir Jenny for siller an' lan'!

He's always compleenin frae mornin to eenin,
  He hoasts an' he hirples the weary day lang;
He's doylt and he's dozin, his blude it is frozen, —
  O dreary's the night wi' a crazy auld man!

He hums and he hankers, he frets and he cankers,
  I never can please him do a' that I can;
He's peevish an' jealous o' a' the young fellows, —
  O dool on the day I met wi' an auld man!

minnie, mother; *siller*, money; *lan'*, land; *hoasts*, coughs; *hirples*, limps; *doylt*, stupid; *dozin*, impotent; *cankers*, complains; *dool*, woe.

My auld auntie Katie upon me taks pity,
  I'll do my endeavour to follow her plan;
I'll cross him an' wrack him, until I heartbreak him
  And then his auld brass will buy me a new pan!

1791

Willie Brew'd a Peck o' Maut*

O Willie brew'd a peck o' maut,
  And Rob and Allan cam to see;
Three blyther hearts, that lee lang night,
  Ye wad na found in Christendie.

        We are na fou, we're nae that fou,
          But just a drappie in our e'e;
        The cock may craw, the day may daw,
          And ay we'll taste the barley bree.

Here are we met, three merry boys,
  Three merry boys I trow are we;
And mony a night we've merry been,
  And mony mae we hope to be!

It is the moon, I ken her horn,
  That's blinkin in the lift sae hie;
She shines sae bright to wyle us hame,
  But by my sooth she'll wait a wee!

Maut, malt; *lee lang*, live long; *fou*, drunk; *drappie*, drop; *e'e*, eye; *bree*, brew; *mony may*, many more; *lift*, sky; *hie*, high; *wyle*, entice; *wee*, bit.

* William Nicol, one of Burns's greatest friends, taught classics at Edinburgh High School. He accompanied the poet on his Highland tour. Allan Masterton was writing master at the High School. The song celebrates a drinking party at Nicol's house in Moffat, 1788. (Ed.)

Wha first shall rise to gang awa,
A cuckold, coward loun is he !
Wha first beside his chair shall fa',
He is the king amang us three !

loun, fellow ; *fa'*, fall.

Whistle o'er the Lave o't

First when Maggy was my care,
Heaven, I thought, was in her air ;
Now we're married, spier nae mair,
But whistle o'er the lave o't.

Meg was meek and Meg was mild,
Sweet and harmless as a child ;
Wiser men than me's beguil'd,
So whistle o'er the lave o't.

How we live, my Meg and me,
How we love and how we gree ;
I carena by how few may see,
Whistle o'er the lave o't.

Wha I wish were maggots meat,
Dish'd up in her winding-sheet ;
I could write — but Meg maun see't,
Whistle o'er the lave o't.

1788

Lave o't, rest of it ; *spier nae mair*, ask no more ; *gree*, agree ; *maun see't*, is
sure to see it.

Merry hae I been Teethin a Heckle

O merry hae I been teethin a heckle,
   An' merry hae I been shapin a spoon:
O merry hae I been cloutin a kettle,
   An' kissin my Katie when a' was done.

O, a' the lang day I ca' at my hammer,
   An' a' the lang day I whistle and sing,
O, a' the lang night I cuddle my kimmer,
   An' a' the lang night as happy's a king.

Bitter in dool I lickit my winnins
   O' marrying Bess, to gie her a slave:
Blest be the hour she cool'd in her linnens,
   And blythe be the bird that sings on her grave!

Come to my arms, my Katie, my Katie,
   An' come to my arms and kiss me again!
Druken or sober here's to thee, Katie!
   And blest be the day I did it again.

hae, have; *Heckle*, flax-comb; *cloutin*, patching; *ca'*, drive; *kimmer*, lass;
dool, sorrow; *lickit my winnins*, tasted my reward; *linnens*, winding-sheet.

A Lass wi' a Tocher

Awa wi' your witchcraft o' Beauty's alarms,
The slender bit beauty you grasp in your arms,
O, gie me the lass that has acres o' charms,
O, gie me the lass wi' the weel-stockit farms!

Tocher, dowry; *bit*, little.

          Then hey, for a lass wi' a tocher,
          Then hey, for a lass wi' a tocher;
          Then hey, for a lass wi' a tocher;
             The nice yellow guineas for me.

Your Beauty's a flower in the morning that blows,
And withers the faster, the faster it grows:
But the rapturous charm o' the bonie green knowes,
Ilk spring they're new deckit wi' bonie white yowes.

And e'en when this Beauty your bosom hath blest,
The brightest o' Beauty may cloy when possess'd;
But the sweet, yellow darlings wi' Geordie impress'd,
The langer ye hae them, the mair they're carest.

                                                    1790

    knowes, knolls, hillocks; *yowes*, ewes; *mair*, more.

Had I the Wyte?

          Had I the wyte, had I the wyte,
             Had I the wyte? she bade me;
          She watch'd me by the hie-gate side,
             And up the loan she shaw'd me.
          And when I wadna venture in,
             A coward loon she ca'd me:
          Had Kirk an' State been in the gate,
             I'd lighted when she bade me.

          Sae craftilie she took me ben,
             And bade me mak nae clatter;
          "For our ramgunshoch, glum gudeman
             Is o'er ayont the water."

  Wyte, blame; *hie-gate*, highway; *loan*, lane; *shaw'd*, showed; *loon*, lad; *ca'd*,
  called; *lighted*, I would have dismounted; *ben*, in; *ramgunshoch*, surly.

Whae'er shall say I wanted grace,
　　When I did kiss and dawt her,
Let him be planted in my place,
　　Syne say I was the fautor!

Could I for shame, could I for shame,
　　Could I for shame refus'd her?
And wadna manhood been to blame,
　　Had I unkindly used her?
He claw'd her wi' the ripplin-kame,
　　And blae and bluidy bruis'd her;
When sic a husband was frae hame,
　　What wife but wad excus'd her!

I dighted aye her e'en sae blue,
　　An' bann'd the cruel randy,
And weel I wat, her willin mou
　　Was sweet as sugar-candie.
At gloamin-shot, it was I wot,
　　I lighted on the Monday;
But I cam thro' the Tyseday's dew,
　　To wanton Willie's brandy.

dawt, pet; *Syne*, then; *fautor*, offender; *claw'd*, scratched; *ripplin-kame*, flax comb; *blae*, blue; *sic*, such; *dighted*, wiped; *aye*, over and over again; *bann'd*, cursed; *randy*, ruffian; *wat*, know; *mou*, mouth; *gloamin-shot*, nightfall; *lighted*, dismounted.

O, for Ane and Twenty, Tam!

An O, for ane and twenty Tam!
　　An hey, sweet ane & twenty, Tam!
I'll learn my kin a rattlin sang,
　　An I saw ane and twenty, Tam.

129   B.P.S.

They snool me sair, & haud me down,
  And gar me look like bluntie, Tam;
But three short years will soon wheel roun',
  And then comes ane & twenty, Tam.

A gleib o' lan', a claut o' gear,
  Was left me by my Auntie, Tam;
At kith or kin I need na spier,
  An I saw ane and twenty, Tam.

They'll hae me wed a wealthy coof,
  Tho' I mysel hae plenty, Tam;
But hearst thou, laddie, there's my loof,
  I'm thine at ane and twenty, Tam!

1791

snool, snub; *sair*, horribly; *haud*, hold; *gar*, make; *bluntie*, stupid; *gleib*,
piece; *lan'*, land; *claut o' gear*, handful of money; *At*, of; *spier*, ask; *coof*,
fool; *loof*, hand.

O Whistle, and I'll Come to You, My Lad

O whistle, and I'll come to you, my lad,
O whistle, and I'll come to you, my lad;
Tho' father and mother and a' should gae mad,
O whistle, and I'll come to you, my lad.

But warily tent, when ye come to court me,
And come na unless the back-yett be a-jee;
Syne up the back-style, and let naebody see,
And come, as ye were na coming to me.
And come, as ye were na coming to me.

tent, watch; *yett*, gate; *a-jee*, ajar; *Syne*, then.

At kirk, or at market, whene'er ye meet me,
Gang by me as tho' that ye car'd nae a flie;
But steal me a blink o' your bonie black e'e,
Yet look as ye were na looking at me,
Yet look as ye were na looking at me.

Ay vow and protest that ye carena for me,
And *whyles* ye may lightly my beauty a wee;
But court nae anither, tho' joking ye be,
For fear that she wyle your fancy frae me,
For fear that she wyle your fancy frae me.

1793

flie, fly; *carena*, care not; *whyles*, sometimes; *lightly*, disparage; *a wee*, a bit.

The Banks o' Doon

Ye Banks and braes o' bonie Doon,
    How can ye bloom sae fresh and fair;
How can ye chant, ye little birds,
    And I sae weary fu' o' care!
Thou'll break my heart thou warbling bird,
    That wanton's thro' the flowering thorn:
Thou minds me o' departed joys,
    Departed never to return.

Oft hae I rov'd by bonie Doon,
    To see the rose and woodbine twine;
And ilka bird sang o' its luve,
    And fondly sae did I o' mine.
Wi' lightsome heart I pu'd a rose,
    Fu' sweet upon its thorny tree;
And my fause luver staw my rose,
    But, ah! he left the thorn wi' me.

1791

ilka, every; *sae*, so; *pu'd*, pulled; *fause*, false; *staw*, stole.

Ca' the Yowes to the Knowes

Ca' the yowes to the knowes,
Ca' them whare the heather growes,
Ca' them whare the burnie rowes,
    My bonie dearie.

Hark, the mavis' evening sang
Sounding Clouden's woods amang;
Then a-faulding let us gang,
    My bonie dearie.

We'll gae down by Clouden side,
Thro' the hazels spreading wide,
O'er the waves, that sweetly glide
    To the moon sae clearly.

Yonder Clouden's silent towers,
Where at moonshine midnight hours,
O'er the dewy bending flowers,
    Fairies dance sae cheary.

Ghaist nor bogle shalt thou fear;
Thou'rt to love and heaven sae dear,
Nocht of ill may come thee near,
    My bonie dearie.

Fair and lovely as thou art,
Thou hast stown my very heart;
I can die — but canna part,
    My bonie dearie.

1788

Ca', drive; *Yowes*, ewes; *Knowes*, knolls; *burnie rowes*, brook runs;
mavis, thrush; *a-faulding*, a-folding; *Ghaist*, ghost; *bogle*, bogy; *sae*, so;
stown, stolen.

A Red, Red Rose

O, my Luve's like a red, red rose,
  That's newly sprung in June.
O, my Luve's like the melodie
  That's sweetly play'd in tune.

As fair art thou, my bonie lass,
  So deep in luve am I;
And I will love thee still, my dear,
  Till a' the seas gang dry.

Till a' the seas gang dry, my dear,
  And the rocks melt wi' the sun:
I will love thee still, my dear,
  While the sands o' life shall run:

And fare thee weel, my only luve!
  And fare thee weel, a while!
And I will come again, my luve,
  Tho' it ware ten thousand mile!

Ae Fond Kiss

Ae fond kiss, and then we sever;
Ae farewell and then for ever!
Deep in heart-wrung tears I'll pledge thee,
Warring sighs and groans I'll wage thee.
Who shall say that fortune grieves him
While the star of hope she leaves him?
Me, nae chearfu' twinkle lights me;
Dark despair around benights me.

I'll ne'er blame my partial fancy,
Naething could resist my Nancy:*
But to see her, was to love her;
Love but her, and love for ever.
Had we never lov'd sae kindly,
Had we never lov'd sae blindly,
Never met — or never parted,
We had ne'er been broken-hearted.

Fare thee weel, thou first and fairest!
Fare thee weel, thou best and dearest!
Thine be ilka joy and treasure,
Peace, enjoyment, love and pleasure!
Ae fond kiss, and then we sever;
Ae fareweel, Alas! for ever!
Deep in heart-wrung tears I'll pledge thee,
Warring sighs and groans I'll wage thee.

1791

* Agnes Maclehose, "Clarinda". (Ed.)

My Bonnie Mary

Go, fetch to me a pint o' wine,
    And fill it in a silver tassie;
That I may drink before I go
    A service to my bonie lassie.
The boat rocks at the Pier o' Leith,
    Fu' loud the wind blaws frae the Ferry,
The ship rides by the Berwick-law,
    And I maun leave my bony Mary.

The trumpets sound, the banners fly,
    The glittering spears are ranked ready,
The shouts o' war are heard afar,
    The battle closes deep and bloody:

It's not the roar o' sea or shore,
   Wad mak me langer wish to tarry;
Nor shouts o' war that's heard afar,
   It's leaving thee, my bony Mary!

1788

The Lovely Lass of Inverness

The lovely lass o' Inverness,
   Nae joy nor pleasure can she see;
For e'en and morn she cries, Alas!
   And ay the saut tear blins her e'e.
Drumossie moor, Drumossie day,
   A waefu' day it was to me;
For there I lost my father dear,
   My father dear and brethren three.

Their winding sheet the bludy clay,
   Their graves are growing green to see;
And by them lies the dearest lad
   That ever blest a woman's e'e!
Now wae to thee thou cruel lord,
   A bludy man I trow thou be;
For mony a heart thou has made sair
   That ne'er did wrang to thine or thee!

1794

saut, salt; *blins*, blinds; *e'e*, eye; *Drumossie moor*, Culloden; *waefu'*, woeful;
sair, sore.

It was A' for Our Rightfu' King

It was a' for our rightfu' king
    We left fair Scotland's strand;
It was a' for our rightfu' king,
    We e'er saw Irish land, my dear,
      We e'er saw Irish land.

Now a' is done that men can do,
    And a' is done in vain:
My Love and Native Land fareweel,
    For I maun cross the main, my dear,
      For I maun cross the main.

He turn'd him right and round about,
    Upon the Irish shore,
And gae his bridle reins a shake,
    With, adieu for evermore, my dear,
      With, adieu for evermore!

The soger frae the wars returns,
    The sailor frae the main,
But I hae parted frae my Love,
    Never to meet again, my dear,
      Never to meet again.

When day is gane, and night is come,
    And a' folk bound to sleep;
I think on him that's far awa,
    The lee-lang night, & weep, my dear,
      The lee-lang night & weep.

1794

gae, gave; *soger*, soldier; *lee-lang*, live-long.

O, wert Thou in the Cauld Blast*

Oh wert thou in the cauld blast,
   On yonder lea, on yonder lea;
My plaidie to the angry airt,
   I'd shelter thee, I'd shelter thee:
Or did misfortune's bitter storms
   Around thee blaw, around thee blaw,
Thy bield should be my bosom,
   To share it a', to share it a'.

Or were I in the wildest waste,
   Sae black and bare, sae black and bare,
The desart were a paradise,
   If thou wert there, if thou wert there.
Or were I monarch o' the globe,
   Wi' thee to reign, wi' thee to reign;
The brightest jewel in my crown,
   Wad be my queen, wad be my queen.

Cauld, cold; *airt*, quarter; *blaw*, blow; *bield*, shelter.

* Written for Jessie Lewars who was nursing the poet during his last illness, 1796. (Ed.)

Of A' the Airts*

OR

I LOVE MY JEAN

Of a' the airts the wind can blaw,
   I dearly like the west,
For there the bony Lassie lives,
   The Lassie I lo'e best:

airt, direction, quarter; *blaw*, blow.

* Written at Ellisland for Jean Armour, the poet's wife, 1793. (Ed.)

There's wild-woods grow, and rivers row,
  And mony a hill between;
But day and night my fancy's flight
  Is ever wi' my Jean.

I see her in the dewy flowers,
  I see her sweet and fair;
I hear her in the tunefu' birds,
  I hear her charm the air:
There's not a bony flower, that springs,
  By fountain, shaw, or green,
There's not a bony bird that sings
  But minds me o' my Jean.

row, flow; *shaw*, wood.

Duncan Gray

Duncan Gray cam here to woo,
  Ha, ha, the wooing o't,
On blythe yule night when we were fu',
  Ha, ha, the wooing o't,
Maggie coost her head fu' high,
Look'd asklent and unco skeigh,
Gart poor Duncan stand abiegh;
  Ha, ha, the wooing o't.

Duncan fleech'd, and Duncan pray'd;
  Ha, ha, the wooing o't,
Meg was deaf as Ailsa Craig,*
  Ha, ha, the wooing o't,

yule, Christmas Eve; *fu'*, drunk; *coost*, tossed; *asklent*, sideways; *unco skeigh*, very skittish; *Gart*, made; *abiegh*, off; *fleech'd*, wheedled.

* An island rock in the Firth of Clyde.

Duncan sigh'd baith out and in,
Grat his een baith bleer't and blin',
Spak o' lowpin o'er a linn;
   Ha, ha, the wooing o't.

Time and chance are but a tide,
   Ha, ha, the wooing o't,
Slighted love is sair to bide,
   Ha, ha, the wooing o't,
Shall I, like a fool, quoth he,
For a haughty hizzie die?
She may gae to — France for me!
   Ha, ha, the wooing o't.

How it comes let doctors tell,
   Ha, ha, the wooing o't,
Meg grew sick — as he grew heal,
   Ha, ha, the wooing o't,
Something in her bosom wrings,
For relief a sigh she brings;
And O, her een, they spak sic things!
   Ha, ha, the wooing o't.

Duncan was a lad o' grace,
   Ha, ha, the wooing o't,
Maggie's was a piteous case,
   Ha, ha, the wooing o't,
Duncan could na be her death,
Swelling pity smoor'd his wrath;
Now they're crouse and canty baith.
   Ha, ha, the wooing o't.

1792

baith, both; *Grat*, wept; *een*, eyes; *Spak*, spoke; *lowpin*, leaping; *linn*,
waterfall; *sair*, hard to; *bide*, endure; *hizzie*, hussy; *heal*, hale; *smoor'd*,
smothered; *crouse*, cheerful; *canty*, merry.

Auld Lang Syne

Should auld acquaintance be forgot
  And never brought to mind?
Should auld acquaintance be forgot,
  And auld lang syne!

        For auld lang syne, my dear,
          For auld lang syne,
        We'll tak a cup o' kindness yet
          For auld lang syne.

And surely ye'll be your pint stowp!
  And surely I'll be mine!
And we'll tak a cup o' kindness yet,
  For auld lang syne.

We twa hae run about the braes,
  And pou'd the gowans fine;
But we've wander'd mony a weary fitt,
  Sin auld lang syne.

We twa hae paidl'd in the burn,
  Frae morning sun till dine;
But seas between us braid hae roar'd,
  Sin auld lang syne.

And there's a hand, my trusty fiere!
  And gie's a hand o' thine!
And we'll tak a right gude-willie waught,
  For auld lang syne.

                                                    1788

be . . . stowp, pay for your own drink; *pou'd*, pulled; *gowans*, daisies; *fitt*, foot; *Sin*, since; *paidl'd*, waded; *dine*, dinner time; *braid*, broad; *fiere*, companion; *gie's*, give me; *gude-willie waught*, friendship (goodwill) drink.

The Patriarch

As honest Jacob on a night,
   Wi' his beloved beauty,
Was duly laid on wedlock's bed,
   And noddin' at his duty.
                 Tal de dal, etc:
"How lang, she says, ye fumblin' wretch,
   Will ye be f—g at it?
My eldest wean might die of age,
   Before that ye could get it.

"Ye pegh and grane, and groazle there,
   And mak an unco splutter,
And I maun ly and thole you here,
   And fient a hair the better."

Then he, in wrath, put up his graith,
   "The deevil's in the hizzie!
I mowe you as I mowe the lave,
   And night and day I'm bisy.

"I've bairn'd the servant gypsies baith,
   Forbye your titty Leah;
Ye barren jad, ye put me mad,
   What mair can I do wi you.

"There's ne'er a mowe I've gi'en the lave,
   But ye ha'e got a dizzen;
And d—n'd a ane ye'se get again,
   Although your c—t should gizzen."

wean, child; *pegh*, puff; *grane*, groan; *groazle*, grunt; *unco*, portentous; *thole*, endure; *fient*, devil; *graith*, gear; *hizzie*, hussy; *lave*, rest; *baith*, both; *Forbye*, besides; *titty*, sister; *jad*, jade; *gi'en*, given; *dizzen*, dozen; *gizzen*, dry up.

Then Rachel calm, as ony lamb,
    She claps him on the waulies:
Quo' she, "ne'er fash a woman's clash,
    In trowth ye mowe me braulies."

"My dear 'tis true, for mony a mowe,
    I'm your ungratefu' debtor,
But ance again, I dinna ken,
    We'll aiblens happen better."

Then honest man! wi' little wark,
    He soon forgat his ire;
The patriarch, he coost the sark,
    And up and till't like fire!

November 1786

waulies, buttocks; *fash*, worry about; *clash*, chatter; *braulies*, fine; *ance*, once; *aiblens*, maybe; *wark*, work; *coost*, cast off; *sark*, shirt; *till't*, tilled.

The Bonniest Lass

The bonniest lass that ye meet neist
    Gie her a kiss an' a' that,
In spite o' ilka parish priest,
    Repentin' stool, and a' that.

            For a' that an' a' that,
                Their mim-mou'd sangs an' a' that,
            In time and place convenient,
                They'll do't themselves for a' that.

Your patriarchs in days o' yore,
    Had their handmaids an' a' that,
O' bastard gets, some had a score
    An' some had mair than a' that.

neist, next; *ilka*, every; *mim-mou'd*, mealy-mouthed; *gets*, brats.

142

For a' that an' a' that,
    Your langsyne saunts, an' a' that,
Were fonder o' a bonie lass,
    Than you or I, for a' that.

King Davie, when he waxèd auld,
    An's bluid ran thin, an' a' that,
An' fand his cods were growin' cauld,
    Could not refrain, for a' that.

    For a' that an' a' that,
        To keep him warm an' a' that,
    The daughters o' Jerusalem
        Were waled for him, an' a' that.

Wha wadna pity thae sweet dames
    He fumbled at, an' a' that,
An' raised their bluid up into flames
    He couldna drown, for a' that.

    For a' that an' a' that:
        He wanted pith, an' a' that:
    For, as to what we shall not name,
        What could he do but claw that.

King Solomon, prince o' divines,
    Wha proverbs made, an' a' that,
Baith mistresses an' concubines
    In hundreds had, for a' that.

    For a' that an' a' that,
        Tho' a preacher wise an' a' that,
    The smuttiest sang that e'er was sung
        His Sang o' Sangs is a' that.

langsyne saunts, saints of long ago; *An's*, and his; *fand*, found; *waled*,
picked; *claw*, fondle or scratch.

Then still I swear, a clever chiel
   Should kiss a lass, an' a' that,
Tho' priests consign him to the deil,
   As reprobate, an' a' that.

     For a' that an' a' that,
       Their canting stuff, an' a' that,
       They ken nae mair wha's reprobate
       Than you or I, for a' that.

Godly Girzie

The night it was a haly night,
   The day had been a haly day;
Kilmarnock gleamed wi' candle light,
   As Girzie hameward took her way.
A man o' sin, ill may he thrive!
   And never haly-meeting see!
Wi' godly Girzie met belyve,
   Amang the Cragie hills sae hie.

The chiel was wight, the chiel was stark,
   He wad na wait to chap nor ca',
And she was faint wi' haly wark,
   She had na pith to say him na.
But ay she glowr'd up to the moon,
   And ay she sigh'd most piouslie;
"I trust my heart's in heaven aboon,
   "Whare'er your sinfu' p——e be."

haly, holy; *belyve*, presently, by and by; *wight*, brisk; *stark*, strong; *chap*,
knock; *ca'*, call; *wark*, work; *pith*, strength; *glowr'd*, gazed; *aboon*, above.

144

Wha'll Mow Me, now?

Tune: "Comin' thro' the rye"

O, I hae tint my rosy cheek,
  Likewise my waste sae sma';
O wae gae by the sodger lown,
  The sodger did it a'.

> O wha'll mow me now, my jo,
>   An' wha'll mow me now:
> A sodger wi' his bandileers
>   Has bang'd my belly fu'.

Now I maun thole the scornfu' sneer
  O' mony a saucy quine;
When, curse upon her godly face!
  Her c——t's as merry's mine.

Our dame hauds up her wanton tail,
  As due as she gaes lie;
An' yet misca's a young thing,
  The trade if she but try.

Our dame can lae her ain gudeman,
  An' mow for glutton greed;
An' yet misca' a poor thing,
  That's mowin' for its bread.

Alake! sae sweet a tree as love,
  Sic bitter fruit should bear!
Alake, that e'er a merry a——e,
  Should draw a sa'tty tear.

tint, lost; *wae gae by*, woe to; *lown*, lad; *maun thole*, must bear; *quine*, wench; *hauds*, holds; *As due . . .*, whenever she lies down; *misca'*, abuse; *Sic*, so; *sa'tty*, salty.

But deevil damn the lousy loon,
    Denies the bairn he got !
Or lea's the merry a—e he lo'ed,
    To wear a ragged coat !

loon, fellow ; *lea's*, leaves ; *lo'ed*, loved.

Nine Inch will Please a Lady

"Come rede me, dame, come tell me, dame,
    My dame come tell me truly,
What length o' graith, when weel ca'd hame,
    Will sair a woman duly?"
The carlin clew her wanton tail,
    Her wanton tail sae ready —
I learn'd a sang in Annandale,
    Nine inch will please a lady. —

But for a koontrie c—nt like mine,
    In sooth, we're nae sae gentle ;
We'll tak tway thumb-bread to the nine,
    And that's a sonsy p—ntle :
O leeze me on my Charlie lad*
    I'll ne'er forget my Charlie !
Tway roarin handfu's and a daud,
    He nidge't it in fu' rarely. —

But weary fa' the laithron doup,
    And may it ne'er be thrivin !

rede, advise ; *graith*, gear ; *ca'd*, driven ; *sair*, serve ; *carlin*, old woman ;
koontrie, country ; *tway thumb-bread*, two thumb breadths ; *sonsy*, hearty ;
daud, lump ; *weary fa'*, curses on ; *laithron doup*, lazy rump.

   * *Leeze me on* : Untranslatable expression denoting great pleasure in or
affection for a person or thing.

It's no the length that maks me loup,
    But it's the double drivin. —
Come nidge me, Tam, come nudge me, Tam,
    Come nidge me o'er the nyvel !
Come lowse & lug your battering ram,
    And thrash him at my gyvel !

loup, leap ; *nyvel*, navel ; *lowse*, let loose ; *gyvel*, gable.

*Had I the Wyte?**

Had I the wyte, had I the wyte,
    Had I the wyte she bad me ;
For she was steward in the house,
    And I was fit-man laddie ;
And when I wadna do't again,
    A silly coof she ca'd me ;
She straik'd my head, and clapt my cheeks,
    And lous'd my breeks and bad me.

Could I for shame, could I for shame,
    Could I for shame deny'd her ;
Or in the bed was I to blame,
    She bad me lye beside her :
I pat six inches in her wame,
    A quarter wadna fly'd her ;
For ay the mair I ca'd it hame,
    Her ports they grew the wider.

My tartan plaid, when it was dark,
    Could I refuse to share it ;

Wyte, blame ; *bad*, ordered ; *steward*, housekeeper ; *fit-man*, footman ;
straik'd, stroked ; *clapt*, patted ; *lous'd*, loosened ; *pat*, put ; *wame*, belly ;
quarter, quarter-yard = 9 inches ; *fly'd*, dismayed ; *ca'd*, drove ; *ports*, gates.

* Compare with the drawing-room version on p. 128. (Ed.)

She lifted up her holland-sark,
    And bad me fin' the gair o't:
Or how could I amang the garse,
    But gie her hilt and hair o't;
She clasped her houghs about my a—e,
    And ay she glowr'd for mair o't.

holland-sark, linen shift; *fin'*, find; *gair*, gusset; *garse*, grass; *gie*, give; *houghs*, thighs; *glowr'd*, looked; *mair*, more.

The Trogger

As I cam down by Annan side,
    Intending for the border,
Amang the Scroggie banks and braes
    Wha met I but a trogger.
He laid me down upon my back,
    I thought he was but jokin',
Till he was in me to the hilts,
    O the deevil tak sic troggin!

What could I say, what could I do,
    I bann'd and sair misca'd him.
But whiltie-whaltie gaed his a—e,
    The mair that I forbade him:
He stell'd his foot against a stane,
    And doubl'd ilka stroke in,
Till I gaed daft amang his hands,
    O the deevil tak sic troggin!

Then up we raise, and took the road,
    And in by Ecclefechan,

Trogger, pedlar; *sic*, such; *bann'd*, cursed; *misca'd*, abused; *whiltie-whaltie*, bumpity-bump; *mair*, more; *stell'd*, braced; *stane*, stone; *ilka*, each; *gaed*, went.

Where the brandy-stoup we gart it clink,
  And the strang-beer ream the quech in.
Bedown the bents o' Bonshaw braes,
  We took the partin' yokin';
But I've claw'd a sairy c——t sinsyne,
  O the deevil tak sic troggin!

gart, made; *ream*, foam in the tankard; *bents*, moor-grass; *yokin'*, bout;
claw'd, stroked; *sairy*, sore.

John Anderson, My Jo*

John Anderson, my jo, John,
  I wonder what ye mean,
To lie sae lang i' the mornin',
  And sit sae late at e'en?
Ye'll bleer a' your een, John,
  And why do ye so?
Come sooner to your bed at e'en,
  John Anderson, my jo.

John Anderson, my jo, John,
  When first that ye began,
Ye had as guid a tail-tree,
  As ony ither man;
But now it's waxen wan, John,
  And wrinkles to and fro:
I've twa gae-ups for ae gae-down,
  John Anderson, my jo.

Jo, joy, dear.

* This is the original version, collected by Burns and preserved in
The Merry Muses of Caledonia, which he "purified" into the famous
sentimental ballad of the same name (see p. 123). However different
in expression, the sentiments are surely the same in kind. (Ed.)

149

I'm backit like a salmon,
  I'm breastit like a swan;
My wame it is a down-cod,
  My middle ye may span:
Frae my tap-knot to my tae, John,
  I'm like the new-fa'n snow;
And it's a' for your convenience,
  John Anderson, my jo.

O it is a fine thing
  To keep out owre the dyke;
But it's a meikle finer thing,
  To see your hurdies fyke;
To see your hurdies fyke, John,
  And hit the rising blow;
It's then I like your chanter-pipe,
  John Anderson, my jo.

When ye come on before, John,
  See that ye do your best;
When ye begin to haud me,
  See that ye grip me fast;
See that ye grip me fast, John,
  Until that I cry "Oh!"
Your back shall crack or I do that,
  John Anderson, my jo.

John Anderson, my jo, John,
  Ye're welcome when ye please;
It's either in the warm bed
  Or else aboon the claes:
Or ye shall hae the horns, John,
  Upon your head to grow;
An' that's the cuckold's mallison,
  John Anderson, my jo.

wame, belly; *down-cod,* feather pillow; *middle,* waist; *tae,* toe; *fa'n,* fallen; *keep out,* watch out; *dyke,* wall; *meikle,* much; *hurdies,* buttocks; *fyke,* busy; *haud,* hold; *aboon,* above; *claes,* bedclothes; *mallison,* curse.

INDEX OF FIRST LINES

Index of First Lines